THE AUSTRALIAN
Women's Weekly

Let me share a secret with you. It's how to eat delicious food that's easy to make, good for your health and guaranteed to whittle down your waistline. I've learned the secret from *The Australian Women's Weekly's* Test Kitchen Director Pamela Clark who, in the past seven months, despite constant temptations and testing of all things fabulous and fattening, has managed to lose an amazing 20 kilos. After 30 years of triple-testing and overseeing *The Weekly's* food, Pamela had got to the stage where nothing fitted her anymore, and she needed to lose some weight before Christmas. Knowing that quick-fix diets never work, and drawing on her vast knowledge of food, she devised a low-carb, low-fat eating plan that has since been tried and tested by many of us magazine girls (and guys), and proven to be most effective. Not only does it work, but the food is absolutely delicious – fresh and easy to prepare. This book is filled with Pamela's inspiring low-carb, low-fat recipes. Thanks to her great ideas, innovative use of herbs and spices as well as fresh produce, you will feel like you're at a dinner party every night. I do. And, best of all, the weight is dropping off. I'm never hungry, and the recipes are easily adapted to suit my family – I simply add rice, potatoes or pasta and everybody's happy. So, if you want to lose weight while eating fabulous food that you can adapt for the whole family and never go hungry, I invite you to share Pamela's diet secrets and recipes.

Deborah Thomas

Deborah Thomas

Editor, *The Australian Women's Weekly*

contents

it works for me

I've lost a total of 20 kilos in 31 weeks, have gone from a size 18 to a size 12 and feel fantastic. Without doubt, this is the easiest diet I have ever followed and, like a lot of you, I've been on so many; I have made yo-yo dieting an art form.

After 31 weeks, I've achieved my target weight loss of 20 kilos and am feeling terrific.

SIX MONTHS PREVIOUSLY...

I have been on this diet for 32 days, in which time I have lost just under seven kilos. All I've done is delete bread, rice, pasta and noodles from my diet – anything that contains processed grains. I've also cut down on starchy root vegetables and pulses, but not eliminated them. I haven't become bored or lost heart. I feel really healthy, have more energy, and am sleeping well.

Strictly speaking, this is not a low-carb diet, I've only restricted certain carbohydrates. Also, the diet is quite low in fat.

I eat mounds of fruit and vegies every day, the fruit in particular is loaded with carbs, the vegies less so. It's important to eat a variety of fruit and vegies to make sure you're getting all the vitamins and minerals you need. Eat whatever is in season; it is cheaper and tastes better.

MY DIETING HISTORY

Apart from following most of the diets ever published, I've done juice and water fasts and even toyed with vegetarianism – a great way to eat, but an impossible regime for me to follow, given my career choice.

Every single diet or eating regime I have ever followed has failed for me when I have gone off the diet. I always, always, always put the weight back on – usually with a few more kilos as a bonus.

I've read all I could about dieting, always looking for the easy, lazy way out, just like I was always on the lookout for an outfit that would make me look younger, thinner and taller. The fact is, I ate too much and exercised too little. And because I chose an industry where I was surrounded by food every day, the odds of me ever being slim were stacked against me from the start.

THE REASONS FOR MY DIET

There were three reasons I felt I had to do something about my weight.

First, I couldn't bear the indigestion I was starting to experience. Secondly, I was staying with friends in the country last year, and one said he wanted to lose a stone (about six kilos) before Christmas. That made me want to lose weight, too. And, lastly, *The Australian Women's Weekly*'s 70th birthday was on the agenda, and there was to be a big party to which I was invited. What on earth was I going to wear?

Nothing much in the wardrobe fitted any more, and I really didn't have the time or the inclination to buy anything. The fact is, I had blossomed. Then I thought, I have three weeks before the party. Even if I lose only a few kilos, that green lacy top I've had for ages would fit and, with the trusty black pants I have in a variety of sizes, that would do.

WHY A LOW-CARB DIET?

The main reason is I've tried all the other diets and failed. But, being curious about all food-related issues, I was interested to see how the low-carb approach would work for me. I know a bit about food, having worked in the industry for more than 40 years, so who better than me to give this diet a whirl?

There are so many diets around, it boggles the mind. Before you embark on any diet, you must have yourself checked over by a doctor. Have your blood pressure and cholesterol levels checked, and be guided by your doctor's advice.

I have a problem with the notion of eating a high-fat, high-protein diet, without fruit and vegetables. It is contrary to everything I know and understand about how food makes you feel. So, I decided I'd simply drop the grain-based food, and not worry about the rest of the food I ate. I lost over four kilos in those first three weeks, so I thought, why not continue?

WEEK BY WEEK

It's Christmas Day, I've been on my diet for 14 weeks and have lost 11 kilos. I've done Christmas dinner without grains and feel great.

Back in the office after Christmas, people begin to comment on my weight loss. Now I'm committed to the diet whether I like it or not because of this book, but that's okay, I'm still well and happy.

By the end of February, the weight loss has slowed down and I've been stuck around the 15-kilo mark for four weeks now. The good news is, I have dropped two dress sizes. My aim is to lose 20 kilos in total over 31 weeks, so I've got eight weeks to go. The funny thing is that I don't have cravings for sweet or fatty foods at all. It's a bonus I didn't expect.

1. My mum (aged 22) and me at two years of age at Balmoral Beach, Sydney. 2. A classic studio shot from the 1940s; I was four and my sister, Toni, was about six months old. 3. Me, aged about three. 4. Another studio shot; I was about two years old. 5. My sister, Sue, aged nine months, and me, aged eight.

With my son, Robby,
daughter-in-law,
Justine, and
granddaughters,
Isobel and
baby Elspeth.

You have to decide
what suits you and
your lifestyle best.
Work out an eating
plan that will be easy
to achieve, then go
for it. This book is my
plan; it has worked for
me and I'm sure it will
work for you, too.

MY FAMILY HISTORY

Many of you will sympathise with me when I tell you about the eating habits established in my childhood. You could say our lives revolved around the next meal. My mother cooked well, so we had good, large, home-cooked meals every night, not forgetting breakfast, packed lunches and weekend picnics, barbecues, etc.

As a family, we ate large meals. We always ate the evening meal together, mostly it consisted of 'meat and three veg'. We always had dessert of some kind; Mum's apple pies were legendary. My mother bought *Woman's Day* and *The Australian Women's Weekly* every week (in those days it *was* a weekly). Mum always took notice of what was in the papers and magazines; if there was a sniff of an idea about anything being bad for one's health, that was the end of it.

Mum made a curry every couple of weeks; she didn't think they could possibly be good for you but, for the sake of variety, she rallied. The curry was either sausages, served with mashed potato and peas, or best-end lamb neck chops with – you guessed it – apple and sultanas, served with boiled rice. It was made like a fricassée, just sort of greenish.

We ate fish once a week on Friday, usually in the form of salmon (canned, of course) mornay, salmon patties, smoked fish, or fresh fish battered or crumbed and fried – we loved it with Mum's homemade chips and coleslaw. I still love that combination. Rarely, as a special treat, we had takeaway fish and chips bought from the local shop.

Chicken and pork were reserved for Christmas and special occasions, and the meat was always roasted along with lots of vegies. For Sunday lunch, a baked dinner, most often a leg of lamb, was the norm.

Just in case we weren't filled to capacity, there was always bread and spread at every meal. White bread was in fashion, but Mum did graduate to brown (only brown in colour I suspect), then later on to wholemeal, once it was mentioned in the magazines or newspapers. We ate only butter on our bread or toast; Mum regarded margarine with suspicion. The spread was the usual: Vegemite, peanut butter, jam, honey, or golden syrup if my father had anything to do with it.

By today's standards we ate and drank more than a normal amount of fruit and milk. Snack foods, such as chips, lollies and biscuits, were banned. As for soft drinks and cordials, they were the root of all dental evil. Mum usually had a good old boiled fruit cake available, but it was always rationed.

THIS IS NOT A NEW DIET

My nanna battled weight, too. She was a keen cook and influenced me in my career choice. I remember her saying she had to stop eating bread, potatoes, cakes, pastry, etc, because she'd put on weight. In those days, pasta was a new food, except for canned spaghetti; rice was eaten mainly as a dessert; noodles were virtually unheard-of. Nanna was on my diet all those years ago without ever knowing it.

MY WORK HISTORY

I have been in the food industry since I left school in the early 1960s. I worked at St George County Council in Sydney as a cookery demonstrator and teacher. It was a great job, almost like an apprenticeship. I gravitated towards baking, confectionery and jam-making, always fascinated by why things went wrong and how to fix them. After seven years there, I was offered a job in *The Australian Women's Weekly* Test Kitchen (*AWW* TK). I started here in September 1969. In 1976 the first in the series of the now-internationally famous *AWW* cookbooks hit the market.

Working in the *AWW* TK, creating recipes, did nothing for my figure, but I loved it here, and still do. Even though I've been battling weight all my life, I have never lost interest in food, and why things work and fail.

THE *AWW* TEST KITCHEN

The Test Kitchen is a unique place, in an office building in the heart of Sydney. It contains 12 'bays', each set up like a mini domestic kitchen.

The TK creates and tests recipes for *The Australian Women's Weekly*, *Woman's Day* and *The Australian Women's Weekly* cookbooks; this amounts to testing and tasting literally thousands of recipes every year. Team members have varied backgrounds, the common thread being a passion for food, a creative bent, excellent cooking skills and the ability to carefully write the recipes they have created so they can be replicated by you at home. The TK is famous for triple-testing recipes; this is why our work is so respected throughout the world – the recipes do work.

The Test Kitchen team presents food for tastings twice a day. Often six people could have cooked at least three things each for one tasting; that's 18 recipes for us to try in one hit. Small wonder I have a weight problem.

As a result of my peculiar job, I prefer not to eat large meals, but you have to decide what suits you and your lifestyle best. Work out an eating plan that will be easy to achieve, then go for it. This book is my plan; it has certainly worked for me and I'm sure it will work for you, too.

1. Here I am at a work-related function in the mid 1980s, eating as usual. 2. Rehearsing in the Test Kitchen with Mike Gibson for an *Australian Women's Weekly* ad, also in the mid 1980s. 3. Eating my way around the markets of Penang in the early 1990s.

MY DIET IN DETAIL
BREAKFAST

I'm well aware that breakfast is an important meal. However, I don't believe there should be rules about when you must and must not eat. The thought of getting out of bed and eating breakfast immediately does not appeal to me at all. By the time I've wandered aimlessly about the streets in the early morning, walking the dog, plotting and planning the day, then gone home, fed the cat and dog, showered, etc, I'm ready for a really good cup of strong coffee, my only one for the day. After that I feel I'm ready to eat something.

I know not everybody has the luxury of being able to do it my way, but listen to what your body is telling you. I decided I'd try putting off breakfast until I hit the office, or, in the case of the weekends, leave breakfast until around 9am, and I've found this works best for me.

By the time I get to the office, at around 8.30am, I'm beginning to feel a bit peckish; then I eat some fruit, usually a banana and at least one other piece of fruit. Or I have some dried fruit with nuts. Sometimes on the weekend I'll treat myself and have a bit of a fry-up (see page 15) for breakfast.

If you lead a very active life, you should eat an appropriate energy-giving breakfast, one that suits your lifestyle. I sit at a desk for most of the day, and, when I'm not doing that, I'm tasting food in the Test Kitchen. The simple fact is, given my sedentary job, I don't need to eat all that much food.

LUNCH

I usually take a salad to the office each day (see box, opposite). I mix and match ingredients quite a bit. I always squeeze half a lemon or lime over everything, then top it with fresh herbs. Sometimes I add a dollop of yogurt. Every third day I make a mix of coarsely chopped fresh herbs.

Don't be mean with the amount of food you eat, I certainly haven't been, and I've still lost lots of weight. If I feel hungry after my salad, I eat some fruit, fresh or dried, and I eat a handful of nuts every day. I've taken a liking to raw cashews; they are a low-GI food (see page 11) and, although high in oil, and therefore high in kilojoules, they make your digestive system work hard, which in turn burns up kilojoules, and the oil is one of the good mono-unsaturated oils that actually help to lower cholesterol in the body. Pecans are another favourite nut of mine, followed closely by walnuts and almonds. If you crave something sweet, try snacking on muscatels, dates or dried pears.

1. My son, Robby, and me with my friend, Barbara Northwood, (now food editor of *Woman's Day*) at a Christmas party in the 1980s. 2. With my first granddaughter, Isobel, aged about four months. 3. With Isobel at her second birthday party. 4. A thinner me with Robby at about 18 months of age.

THE MAIN MEAL OF THE DAY

In a perfect world, I really believe the main meal of the day should be eaten in the middle of the day, and it should be a relaxed, slowly eaten meal, but then there's reality. I go to work all week, and eat most of the day, but does that stop me from wanting a meal in the evening? Certainly not. So my main meal is in the evening, along with most of the population.

From Monday to Friday I eat a simple meal in the evening, something that is quick and easy to prepare, because I really only want to relax in front of the TV or read a book, just quietly closing down for the night. I always have some form of protein with vegetables or salad, depending on what I ate during the day. I eat fish at least twice a week, usually three times, and I can happily eat my way through a large cutlet or steak of whatever type of fish I fancy.

Chicken thigh fillets or cutlets are another stand-by; I'll eat, grilled or barbecued, one or two pieces, depending on their size.

Once a week, I'll have a steak, rump usually, a decent-sized piece, and I trim the excess fat away before I cook it. Mostly I barbecue it, or cook it in a griddle pan, over a really high heat, until it's barely done, then wrap it in foil to rest before I eat it. Lamb chops, and cutlets of all types, are other favourites. I eat a wide variety of vegetables, usually steamed or stir-fried.

During the weekend I'm likely to cook something more fancy to feed the family. For inspiration, just feast your eyes on the wonderful recipes throughout this book.

If you're the meal-preparer and the only member of the family 'on a diet' you'll know there's no fun in having to prepare different meals for other family members, so all the main courses in this book can be eaten by the non-dieters in the family, and we've suggested what carbs you could add to make the meal more 'normal' (see page 13).

ALCOHOL

Sometimes I have a glass of red or white wine with my main meal, sometimes I have a little more. I have never been much of a drinker. I probably drink alcohol three or four times a week, but who's counting? Do remember that alcohol has almost twice the kilojoules of carbohydrate.

EATING LITTLE AND OFTEN

If this system of grazing works for you, that's great. If you happen to work in a Test Kitchen, you simply have to adjust to being a grazer. I don't really think it's the best way of eating. The poor old digestive system just begins to work on one batch of food when it's hit with yet another batch. It never gets a rest.

MY IDEAL LUNCH

Here's a sample of the sort of things I put into my lunch box:

one large ripe tomato OR half a punnet of grape or cherry tomatoes;

a big handful of rocket leaves, baby spinach or any lettuce OR about two handfuls of finely shredded cabbage;

the following chopped or grated ingredients: half a lebanese cucumber; celery sticks; carrot sticks; radishes; half a red capsicum;

a piece (about 25g) of tasty cheddar cheese (I confess to preferring high-fat cheese) OR half a large (or a small) avocado;

two hard-boiled eggs OR a small can of tuna (I like tuna in oil best) or salmon, OR about 150g cold meat, eg, grilled or poached chicken, grilled lamb cutlets or chops, ham or beef (cooked or corned).

EXERCISE

I'm sure we're all very different in terms of what we need to eat and drink to be healthy; I think the same goes for exercise. I feel so much better if I exercise in a moderate way. I like to walk and swim, but hate someone telling me what I should do in group exercises; as for gyms, I really can't think of anything worse.

Being on this diet has made me more energetic. I hit the floor at 5.30am and take my dog for a walk. If it's raining, I don't go. I refuse to feel guilty about anything to do with diet or exercise.

When I was growing up, people did more of what we grandly call incidental exercise today. My mum didn't drive, she walked to the shops. She carried heavy things; there was no need for walking or running around the streets with weighted backpacks.

Since we don't even get off our chairs to change the TV channel, we have to do something else to keep the body moving. We know that child obesity is on the increase, so somehow we have to make exercising accepted as something we do every day, along with eating and sleeping.

My best advice on this subject is to do what exercise you like to do. If you love yoga, dancing or swimming, do it and enjoy it; don't burden yourself with exercise that feels like a chore, as you won't stick with it.

There is no doubt exercise makes you feel better, and it increases the metabolic rate of your body. So, even though your weight may stay the same for a while, muscle is replacing fat ever so slowly. Muscle is heavier than fat, so be patient, don't give up on either the diet or the exercise. If you measure yourself once a month, you will be staggered by the difference, even if the scales have been reluctant to move in a downward way. Just watch people's jaws drop when you tell them the total centimetres, or even metres, you've lost.

My last word on the subject of exercise is this: if kilojoules gained from food input exceed kilojoules expended from exercise output, you're going to put on weight, it's really as simple as that.

WEIGHT MAINTENANCE

This is the hard bit. I've decided to re-introduce low-GI grain-based foods (carbs) into my diet after I've reached my target weight loss of 20 kilos. The thing about low-GI foods is that they make your body work hard to digest and deal with them (see opposite). This is a good thing – if your digestive system is working hard, it means more kilojoules are being burned up during the process. Try to remember to chew the food you eat really well, as chewing kick-starts the digestive process, giving your body a chance to work properly.

1. My low-carb toasted muesli (see recipe, opposite), topped off with a dollop of yogurt.
2. Home economists Kirrily Smith (left) and Christina Martignago with me at a tasting in the Test Kitchen, March 2004. 3. Kirrily and me, still eating.

LOW-GI FOODS

Certain types of carbohydrates are better for you than others. The glycaemic index (GI) is a way of classifying carbohydrates according to their effect on blood glucose (blood sugar) levels in the body. Carbohydrates that break down slowly and release glucose into the blood stream gradually have a low-GI rating (55 or less), while those that are easily digested and absorbed more quickly have high-GI values (70 or more). Low-GI foods keep you feeling fuller for longer, and keep your energy levels up over longer periods of time, while high-GI foods give your body a rapid energy boost, and you will feel hungry again sooner. Generally, lower GI values are preferable.

The low-GI foods I intend to introduce in small quantities are rice, in particular basmati and Doongara CleverRice (varieties with the lowest GI), slightly undercooked (al dente) pasta, and some good wholegrain bread. When winter comes along I'll be slightly increasing the pulses and starchy root vegetables I eat now. Other than these additions, I intend sticking to this way of eating most of the time.

EATING OUT

I have to eat out quite often at work-related functions. So far I have had no difficulty avoiding grain-based, high-carb foods. Most restaurants are diet-sympathetic these days anyway, so if there is nothing that suits you on the menu, either forget the diet (after all, it's what you do most of the time that matters) or ask the waiter if the chef could re-jig something on the menu for you. If you know when and where you're going to eat, phone ahead, explain your diet, and they'll be sure to help.

Takeaway food is quite another matter. Definitely avoid pizzas, fried fish and chips, burgers, etc. However, there's usually something you can eat on the menu, or deconstruct to suit your needs. Bunless hamburgers are growing in popularity and most fish and chip shops will grill fish for you, so have two pieces of fish with lemon, and avoid the fried chips. If they do salads, have one of those. It's really not hard; just make sensible choices.

EATING A VARIETY OF FOODS

It's important to eat as wide a variety of foods as possible, so you're covering all bases, a bit like an insurance policy taken out for good health. If you eat a lot of different foods, and presuming you're basically healthy, you will not need to spend money on vitamin and mineral supplements while you're on this diet of mine.

toasted muesli

PREPARATION TIME 10 MINUTES
COOKING TIME 10 MINUTES

This muesli is filling, will sustain you, makes you chew, and tastes divine – what more could you want? Eat it with a little skim milk plus a dollop of yogurt. If you want to add fresh or stewed fruit, that's fine too. Store the muesli in an airtight container in the refrigerator for up to three months, and keep a ⅓-cup measure in there, too.

2 tablespoons golden syrup
2 tablespoons walnut oil
1 cup (90g) rolled oats
1 cup (160g) coarsely chopped blanched almonds
1 cup (120g) coarsely chopped roasted hazelnuts
1 cup (160g) pepitas (pumpkin seed kernels)
1⅓ cups (220g) sunflower seed kernels
½ cup (70g) linseed, sunflower and almond blend (LSA)
⅓ cup (55g) finely chopped dried seeded dates
½ cup (75g) finely chopped dried apricots

1 Preheat oven to moderate.
2 Combine syrup and oil in small bowl.
3 Combine oats and nuts in shallow baking dish; drizzle with syrup mixture. Toast, uncovered, in moderate oven about 10 minutes or until browned lightly, stirring halfway through cooking time. Cool 10 minutes.
4 Stir pepitas, kernels, LSA blend and dried fruit into muesli mixture; cool.

serves 20 (⅓ cup per serving)
per serving 11.4g carbohydrate; 21.1g total fat (2.1g saturated fat); 1112kJ (266 cal); 8.6g protein

My weight-loss progress, week by week.

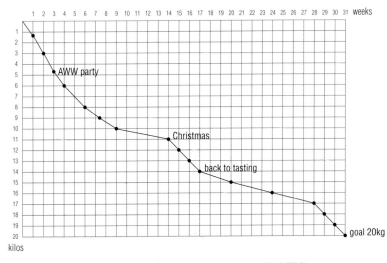

WATER AND SALT

I think you need only drink water when you're thirsty. If you're exercising strenuously, and sweating heavily, you'll feel thirsty – that's when you need to drink, and there's nothing like water to quench your thirst.

If you have become used to eating a lot of highly salted food, try to break the habit, or at least try to reduce the amount of salt you eat; like anything in excess, it isn't healthy.

FATS

It's a fact that we all need fat in our diet; it's the type and amount that causes the arguments. Suffice to say, mono-unsaturated and polyunsaturated fats are the good guys. These are highest in olive, canola, macadamia and peanut oils, avocados, nuts, margarine and seafood (particularly oily fish). Saturated fats, found mostly in animal products (butter, cheese, cream and fatty meats) are the bad guys that tend to raise cholesterol and be deposited as body fat, and these are the ones we need to minimise. This is why saturated fat is itemised in the nutritional information following each recipe in this book.

COUNTING KILOJOULES

I haven't concerned myself with this exercise; how could I, my job involves tasting the weirdest combinations of things at one sitting. I would drive myself crazy if I tried to work out how many kilojoules I got through in a day. It would be a terrifying total, which makes me wonder about kilojoules. It must be that the different types of food and their kilojoules affect my body in different ways.

THE DREADED CRAVINGS

I think I have a sweet tooth. I once told my long-time friend and colleague, Rosemary Stanton, this; she told me I was wrong, that I had a fat tooth, and that it was coincidence the things I craved, such as chocolate and ice-cream, were sweet.

Now, when I fancy something sweet, I head for the dried fruit. I eat a handful each day, often teamed with the handful of nuts I eat daily. I find the fruit and nut mix, eaten slowly, makes me feel satisfied and quite full.

Another oil-rich food that gives me that full, satisfied feeling is avocado. I am mad about this fruit; it's so beneficial to health and is great to eat, too. How good is that? It is one of nature's own multivitamin pills.

A TYPICAL DAY'S MENU

6am: A big mug of strong plunger coffee with 1 teaspoon demerara sugar and a good splash of full-cream milk.

8.30am: Quarter of a rockmelon, chopped into strawberry-sized pieces, plus half a punnet of halved strawberries, topped with the pulp of two passionfruit OR one banana, topped with ⅓ cup yogurt and the pulp of one passionfruit OR ⅓ cup toasted muesli (see box, page 11) with a splash of skim milk and a spoonful of yogurt.

An all-day snack and a drink: A handful (⅓ cup) each of nuts and dried fruit, plus a drink from the selection on pages 112-115.

10am: Two pieces of fresh fruit.

12 noon: Test Kitchen tasting.

1pm: A large salad with two hard-boiled eggs (see box, page 9) plus a cup of tea with a little skim milk.

2pm: Two pieces of fresh fruit.

3pm: Test Kitchen tasting.

7pm: Choose from one of the main-course recipes in this book (see pages 20-111), accompanied by a glass of wine.

REACTIONS TO SOME FOODS

The digestive system is a wonderfully efficient mechanism when it's given the chance to work properly. Mine has always been efficient.

However, as I draw near to my 60th birthday, I have to say that my digestive system is not what it used to be. A year or so ago, for the first time in my life, I learned about indigestion. I asked my doctor about this nasty feeling and, after some basic medical checks and questioning, and quite a bit of eye-rolling, she told me I had indigestion, to buy some antacid, and basically get on with it.

Since day one of my diet, I have not had the slightest sign of indigestion. I can only assume I had been seriously overloading my system with more carbs than my body could possibly handle. Maybe I had got away with this overload in the past because I and my digestive system were younger and stronger. I just don't know, but since dropping the processed grains (carbohydrates) from my diet – not counting the ones I eat at tastings – I'm a new woman. It must be said that almost all of those processed grains were high-GI foods, too.

ADAPTING MY DIET FOR NON-DIETERS

The recipes in this book are really delicious, the flavours are fresh, and the combination of ingredients nutritionally sound. All that is missing, traditionally speaking, is the carbohydrate element. If you're going to add carbs to the recipes for some or all members of the family, think about the type you're adding, and why.

Consider if the people who are going to eat the meals lead sedentary or active lives; don't overload them with energy foods their bodies can't use.

I don't want you to think I am never going to eat carbs again, I am. I really like the starchy textures of grains. I will go slowly when reintroducing them to my diet, and only eat small amounts. It will be enough, as I don't expect my lifestyle or job to change much in the next few years. Try to choose carb foods that are going to make your body work hard to digest them, in other words, choose low-GI foods.

In conclusion, here I am at the end of 31 weeks and I'm delighted to say that I've achieved my target of losing 20 kilos, with as little inconvenience as possible. I'm feeling great and look forward to continuing to eat wisely, without depriving myself of life's little culinary pleasures.

1. With Geoff Jansz in March 2004, filming a segment on the Nine Network's cooking show, *Fresh! Cooking with The Australian Women's Weekly*. 2. At a Test Kitchen tasting in April 2004, with home economists (from left) Kirrily Smith and Nancy Duran.

You can find more information about Pamela's diet and more delicious low-carb recipes in *The Magazine Editors' Diet*, published by ACP Books and available from bookstores and newsagents, priced at $19.95.

breakfast

crisp prosciutto with mango and avocado salsa

PREPARATION TIME 15 MINUTES
COOKING TIME 5 MINUTES

1 medium mango (430g), chopped coarsely
1 large avocado (320g), chopped coarsely
1 small red onion (100g), chopped finely
1 small red capsicum (150g), chopped finely
1 fresh small red thai chilli, chopped finely
2 tablespoons lime juice
8 slices prosciutto (120g), halved lengthways

1 Place mango, avocado, onion, capsicum, chilli and juice in medium bowl; toss salsa to combine.
2 Cook prosciutto in large lightly oiled frying pan until crisp. Serve prosciutto with salsa.

serves 4
per serving 12.2g carbohydrate; 14.7g total fat (3.4g saturated fat); 893kJ (213 cal); 8.2g protein
carb tip Serve with warm corn tortillas.

scrambled eggs with dill and smoked salmon

PREPARATION TIME 5 MINUTES
COOKING TIME 5 MINUTES

8 eggs
½ cup (125ml) milk
1 tablespoon finely chopped fresh dill
10g butter
300g thinly sliced smoked salmon

1 Whisk eggs in medium bowl; add milk and dill, whisk until combined.
2 Melt butter in medium frying pan; cook egg mixture over low heat, stirring gently, until mixture is just set.
3 Serve egg mixture with salmon.

serves 4
per serving 1.8g carbohydrate; 16.8g total fat (5.9g saturated fat); 1179kJ (282 cal); 31.1g protein
carb tip Serve with small buckwheat pancakes, sour cream and finely chopped red onion.

breakfast fry-up

PREPARATION TIME 10 MINUTES

COOKING TIME 20 MINUTES

4 medium egg tomatoes (300g), quartered
2 tablespoons balsamic vinegar
cooking-oil spray
300g mushrooms, sliced thickly
½ cup loosely packed fresh basil leaves, torn
¼ cup loosely packed fresh coriander leaves
¼ cup loosely packed fresh flat-leaf parsley leaves
200g shaved ham

1 Preheat oven to moderately hot.
2 Combine tomato and half of the vinegar in medium shallow oiled baking dish; spray with oil. Roast, uncovered, in moderately hot oven 20 minutes.
3 Cook mushrooms and remaining vinegar in medium oiled frying pan until tender; stir in herbs. Transfer to serving dishes; cover to keep warm.
4 Heat ham in same pan. Serve with mushroom and tomato mixtures.

serves 4
per serving 2.6g carbohydrate; 2.9g total fat
(0.7g saturated fat); 380kJ (91 cal); 13g protein
carb tip Serve with thick slices of toast.

minted fruit salad

PREPARATION TIME 25 MINUTES

COOKING TIME 15 MINUTES (PLUS REFRIGERATION TIME)

1½ cups (375ml) water
1 tablespoon grated palm sugar
2 star anise
2 tablespoons lime juice
1 small pineapple (800g), chopped coarsely
1 small honeydew melon (900g), chopped coarsely
500g fresh lychees, seeded
200g seedless red grapes
½ cup loosely packed fresh mint leaves, torn

1 Stir the water, sugar and star anise in small saucepan over heat until sugar dissolves. Simmer, uncovered, 10 minutes. Stir in juice. Cover; refrigerate 3 hours. Strain syrup into medium jug; discard star anise.
2 Combine fruit, mint and syrup in large bowl.

serves 4
per serving 39.7g carbohydrate; 0.8g total fat
(0g saturated fat); 755kJ (180 cal); 3.7g protein
carb tip Serve with cinnamon-dusted brioche toast.

poached eggs with bacon, spinach and pecorino

PREPARATION TIME 5 MINUTES

COOKING TIME 10 MINUTES

600g spinach, trimmed, chopped coarsely
4 bacon rashers (280g), rind removed
4 eggs
⅓ cup (40g) shaved pecorino cheese

1 Boil, steam or microwave spinach until just wilted; drain. Cover to keep warm.
2 Meanwhile, heat large non-stick frying pan; cook bacon until crisp. Drain on absorbent paper; cover to keep warm.
3 Half-fill the same pan with water; bring to a boil. Break eggs into cup, one at a time, then slide into pan. When all eggs are in pan, allow water to return to a boil. Cover pan, turn off heat; stand about 4 minutes or until a light film of egg white sets over yolks. Remove eggs, one at a time, using slotted spoon; place on absorbent-paper-lined saucer to blot up poaching liquid.
4 Divide spinach among serving plates; top each spinach portion with bacon, egg then cheese.

serves 4
per serving 0.8g carbohydrate; 13.1g total fat (5.2g saturated fat); 813kJ (194 cal); 18.5g protein
carb tip Serve on toasted turkish bread.

egg-white omelette

PREPARATION TIME 25 MINUTES

COOKING TIME 20 MINUTES

12 egg whites
4 green onions, chopped finely
¼ cup finely chopped fresh chives
¼ cup finely chopped fresh chervil
½ cup finely chopped fresh flat-leaf parsley
½ cup (60g) coarsely grated cheddar cheese
½ cup (50g) coarsely grated mozzarella cheese

1 Preheat grill.
2 Beat a quarter of the egg white in small bowl with electric mixer until soft peaks form; fold in a quarter of the combined onion and herbs.
3 Pour mixture into 20cm heated lightly oiled non-stick frying pan; cook, uncovered, over low heat until omelette is just browned lightly on the bottom.
4 Sprinkle a quarter of the combined cheeses on half of the omelette. Place pan under preheated grill until cheese begins to melt and omelette sets; fold omelette over to completely cover cheese. Carefully slide onto serving plate; cover to keep warm.
5 Repeat process three times with remaining egg white, onion and herb mixture, and cheese.

serves 4
per serving 1.1g carbohydrate; 7.9g total fat (5g saturated fat); 620kJ (148 cal); 18.2g protein
carb tip Serve with roast tomatoes and toast.

baked eggs with pancetta

PREPARATION TIME 15 MINUTES

COOKING TIME 20 MINUTES

2 teaspoons olive oil

1 small red capsicum (150g), chopped finely

6 slices pancetta (90g), chopped finely

100g mushrooms, chopped finely

4 green onions, chopped finely

⅔ cup (50g) finely grated parmesan cheese

8 eggs

2 teaspoons coarsely chopped fresh
    flat-leaf parsley

1   Preheat oven to moderately hot. Lightly oil four
    ¾-cup (180ml) ovenproof dishes.
2   Heat oil in medium frying pan; cook capsicum and
    pancetta, stirring, until capsicum is just tender. Add
    mushroom and onion; cook, stirring, until onion just
    softens. Remove from heat; stir in half the cheese.
3   Divide capsicum mixture among dishes; break two
    eggs into each dish. Bake, uncovered, in moderately
    hot oven 5 minutes. Sprinkle remaining cheese over
    eggs; bake, further 5 minutes or until eggs are just
    set. Sprinkle with parsley just before serving.

serves 4

per serving 2.5g carbohydrate; 20g total fat
(7.3g saturated fat); 1187kJ (284 cal); 23.9g protein
carb tip Serve with sliced toasted french bread.

baked ricotta with tomato

PREPARATION TIME 10 MINUTES

COOKING TIME 15 MINUTES

2 teaspoons olive oil

1 tablespoon pine nuts

2 cloves garlic, crushed

100g baby spinach leaves

1¼ cups (250g) low-fat ricotta cheese

1 egg, beaten lightly

2 tablespoons coarsely chopped fresh chives

500g baby vine-ripened truss tomatoes

1 tablespoon balsamic vinegar

1   Preheat oven to hot. Lightly oil four holes of a six-hole
    ⅓-cup (80ml) muffin pan.
2   Heat half of the oil in medium frying pan; cook nuts and
    garlic until fragrant. Add spinach; stir until wilted. Cool.
3   Combine spinach mixture in medium bowl with cheese,
    egg and chives; divide among prepared holes. Bake
    in hot oven about 15 minutes or until browned.
4   Combine tomatoes and vinegar with remaining oil in
    small shallow baking dish. Roast, uncovered, in hot
    oven 10 minutes. Serve baked ricotta with tomatoes.

serves 4

per serving 4g carbohydrate; 11.8g total fat
(4.4g saturated fat); 686kJ (164 cal); 10.5g protein
carb tip Serve with toasted ciabatta.

baked apples with berries

PREPARATION TIME 10 MINUTES

(PLUS REFRIGERATION TIME)

COOKING TIME 45 MINUTES

2 cups (300g) frozen mixed berries
4 large green apples (800g)
4 cardamom pods
½ cup (140g) yogurt
2 teaspoons honey

1 Place berries in fine sieve set over small bowl, cover; thaw in refrigerator overnight.
2 Preheat oven to moderately slow.
3 Core unpeeled apples about three-quarters of the way down from stem end, making hole 4cm in diameter. Use small sharp knife to score around circumference of each apple. Make small deep cut in base of each apple; insert one cardamom pod into each cut.
4 Pack three-quarters of the berries firmly into apples; place apples in small baking dish. Bake, uncovered, in moderately slow oven about 45 minutes or until apples are just tender.
5 Meanwhile, push remaining berries through sieve into small bowl; stir in yogurt and honey.
6 Serve apples with yogurt mixture.

serves 4
per serving 24.5g carbohydrate; 1.4g total fat (0.8g saturated fat); 518kJ (124 cal); 3.4g protein
carb tip Serve with warm croissants.

spiced plums with yogurt

PREPARATION TIME 10 MINUTES

COOKING TIME 10 MINUTES (PLUS COOLING TIME)

1 litre (4 cups) water
½ cup (125ml) orange juice
⅓ cup (75g) caster sugar
5cm strip orange rind
2 star anise
4 cloves
1 teaspoon mixed spice
1 cinnamon stick
1 vanilla bean, split lengthways
8 blood plums (900g), unpeeled
1⅓ cups (375g) yogurt

1 Place the water, juice, sugar, rind and spices in medium frying pan. Scrape vanilla seeds into pan then add pod; cook mixture, stirring, until sugar dissolves.
2 Add plums to pan; poach, uncovered, over low heat about 10 minutes or until just tender. Using slotted spoon, place two plums in each of four serving dishes (reserve 2 tablespoons of the poaching liquid). Cool plums 20 minutes.
3 Combine yogurt and reserved poaching liquid in small bowl; serve with plums.

serves 4
per serving 39.1g carbohydrate; 3.4g total fat (2.1g saturated fat); 906kJ (217 cal); 5.7g protein
carb tip Serve with fruit toast.

tropical fruit salad

PREPARATION TIME 10 MINUTES

COOKING TIME 20 MINUTES (PLUS REFRIGERATION TIME)

2 cups (500ml) water
3 cardamom pods, bruised
4cm piece fresh ginger (20g), quartered
1 teaspoon finely grated lemon rind
1 tablespoon lemon juice
1 tablespoon lime juice
1 vanilla bean, split lengthways
½ medium rockmelon (850g), chopped coarsely
1 small papaya (600g), chopped coarsely
3 medium kiwi fruit (255g), sliced thickly
1 medium mango (430g), chopped coarsely
⅓ cup (80ml) passionfruit pulp

1 Place the water, cardamom, ginger, rind and juices into medium frying pan. Scrape vanilla seeds into pan then add pod; bring to a boil. Reduce heat; simmer, uncovered, without stirring, 20 minutes. Strain syrup into medium jug; discard spices and pod. Cool 10 minutes. Refrigerate, covered, until syrup is cold.
2 Just before serving, place syrup and remaining ingredients in large bowl; toss gently to combine.

serves 4
per serving 30.6g carbohydrate; 0.6g total fat
(0g saturated fat); 607kJ (145 cal); 3.4g protein
carb tip Serve with thick greek-style yogurt.

bacon and asparagus frittata

PREPARATION TIME 15 MINUTES

COOKING TIME 45 MINUTES

4 bacon rashers (280g), rind removed, sliced thickly
1 large red onion (300g), sliced thinly
170g asparagus, trimmed, halved lengthways
4 eggs
4 egg whites
1 cup (250ml) buttermilk

1 Preheat oven to moderate. Oil deep 19cm-square cake pan; line base and sides with baking paper.
2 Cook bacon, stirring, in small heated non-stick frying pan until crisp; drain on absorbent paper. Add onion to same pan; cook, stirring, until soft. Layer bacon, onion and asparagus in prepared pan.
3 Whisk eggs, egg white and buttermilk in medium jug; pour into pan. Bake, uncovered, in moderate oven about 35 minutes or until frittata is set. Stand 10 minutes before cutting into squares.

serves 4
per serving 8.5g carbohydrate; 11.6g total fat
(4.3g saturated fat); 1349kJ (322 cal); 45.6g protein
carb tip Serve with toasted sourdough.

seafood

salade niçoise

PREPARATION TIME 20 MINUTES **COOKING TIME** 10 MINUTES

1 Boil, steam or microwave beans until just tender; drain. Rinse under cold water; drain.
2 Meanwhile, make light vinaigrette.
3 Place tomato, olives, cucumber, onion, mesclun and egg in large bowl with vinaigrette; toss gently to combine. Divide salad among serving plates; flake fish over salad in large chunks.

LIGHT VINAIGRETTE Place ingredients in screw-top jar; shake well.

serves 4
per serving 10.8g carbohydrate; 11.1g total fat (3.2g saturated fat); 1128kJ (269 cal); 31g protein
carb tip Serve with rinsed and drained canned white beans.

200g green beans, trimmed, chopped coarsely
250g cherry tomatoes, halved
½ cup (80g) seeded black olives
2 lebanese cucumbers (260g), sliced thickly
1 medium red onion (170g), sliced thinly
150g mesclun *salad leaves*
6 hard-boiled eggs, quartered
425g can tuna in springwater, drained

LIGHT VINAIGRETTE
1 teaspoon olive oil
¼ cup (60ml) lemon juice
1 clove garlic, crushed
2 teaspoons dijon mustard

hot and sour steamed fish with thai salad

PREPARATION TIME 35 MINUTES (PLUS REFRIGERATION TIME) **COOKING TIME** 10 MINUTES

Always choose a sweetly aromatic mango that has a slight give when squeezed gently. The colour changes as the fruit ripens, from green to yellow-orange or even red.

4 x 200g trevally fillets
3 fresh small red thai chillies, seeded, sliced thinly
3 fresh kaffir lime leaves, shredded finely
10cm stick (20g) fresh lemon grass, chopped finely
½ cup loosely packed fresh coriander leaves
½ cup loosely packed fresh mint leaves
½ cup loosely packed fresh basil leaves
150g snow peas, trimmed, sliced thinly
2 fresh long red chillies, seeded, sliced thinly
2 green onions, sliced thinly
50g snow pea sprouts
1 large mango (600g), sliced thinly

LIME AND SWEET CHILLI DRESSING
2 teaspoons sweet chilli sauce
⅓ cup (80ml) fish sauce
⅓ cup (80ml) lime juice
2 teaspoons peanut oil
1 clove garlic, crushed
1cm piece fresh ginger (5g), grated
1 teaspoon grated palm sugar

1 Make lime and sweet chilli dressing.
2 Combine fish, thai chilli, lime leaf and lemon grass in large bowl with half of the dressing, cover; refrigerate 30 minutes.
3 Place fish mixture, in single layer, in baking-paper-lined large bamboo steamer; steam, covered, over wok or large frying pan of simmering water about 10 minutes or until fish is cooked as desired.
4 Meanwhile, place remaining ingredients in large bowl with remaining dressing; toss gently to combine. Serve fish with salad.

LIME AND SWEET CHILLI DRESSING Place ingredients in screw-top jar; shake well.

serves 4
per serving 19.8g carbohydrate; 8.7g total fat (2.1g saturated fat);
1454kJ (347 cal); 46.5g protein
carb tip Serve with steamed jasmine rice.

Shallots, coriander root and palm sugar are just three of the essential ingredients that go into the making of a classic nam jim, the most well known of all the hot and spicy thai sauces.

poached flathead with nam jim and herb salad

PREPARATION TIME 30 MINUTES **COOKING TIME** 10 MINUTES

8 flathead fillets (1kg)
1 litre (4 cups) water
1 tablespoon fish sauce
1 tablespoon lime juice

NAM JIM
2 cloves garlic, quartered
3 long green chillies, seeded, chopped coarsely
2 coriander roots
2 tablespoons fish sauce
2 tablespoons grated palm sugar
3 shallots (75g), chopped coarsely
⅓ cup (80ml) lime juice
1 tablespoon peanut oil

MIXED HERB SALAD
1½ cups loosely packed fresh mint leaves
1 cup loosely packed fresh coriander leaves
1 cup loosely packed fresh basil leaves, torn
1 medium red onion (170g), sliced thinly
2 lebanese cucumbers (260g), seeded, sliced thinly

1 Make nam jim.
2 Halve each fillet lengthways. Combine the water, sauce and juice in large frying pan; bring to a boil. Add fish, reduce heat; simmer, uncovered, about 5 minutes or until cooked as desired. Remove fish from pan with slotted spoon; cover to keep warm.
3 Meanwhile, make mixed herb salad.
4 Serve fish on salad; top with remaining nam jim.

NAM JIM Blend or process ingredients until smooth.
MIXED HERB SALAD Combine ingredients in medium bowl with a third of the nam jim.

serves 4
per serving 12.2g carbohydrate; 7.6g total fat (1.9g saturated fat); 1458kJ (348 cal); 56.7g protein
carb tip Toss rinsed and drained fresh rice noodles through salad.

prawn, scallop and asparagus salad with ginger dressing

PREPARATION TIME 25 MINUTES **COOKING TIME** 10 MINUTES

400g uncooked medium king prawns

400g sea scallops

250g asparagus, trimmed, halved

⅓ cup coarsely chopped fresh chives

120g baby spinach leaves

1 large red capsicum (350g), chopped coarsely

GINGER DRESSING

5cm piece fresh ginger (25g), grated

1 tablespoon olive oil

2 tablespoons lemon juice

1 teaspoon sugar

1 Shell and devein prawns, leaving tails intact.
2 Cook prawns, scallops and asparagus, in batches, on heated lightly oiled grill plate (or grill or barbecue) until cooked as desired.
3 Meanwhile, make ginger dressing.
4 Place prawns, scallops, asparagus, chives, spinach and capsicum in bowl with dressing; toss gently to combine.

GINGER DRESSING Press grated ginger between two spoons over large bowl to extract juice; discard fibres. Whisk in oil, juice and sugar until combined.

serves 4
per serving 6g carbohydrate; 5.9g total fat (0.9g saturated fat);
749kJ (179 cal); 25g protein
carb tip Serve with warmed ciabatta loaf.

Choose asparagus spears of similar thickness to ensure they cook evenly. One of the most perishable of vegetables, asparagus is best eaten as close to picking time as possible.

barbecued sweet and sour blue-eye

PREPARATION TIME 20 MINUTES **COOKING TIME** 20 MINUTES

1 Cook pineapple, capsicums and red onion on heated lightly oiled grill plate (or grill or barbecue) until browned all over and tender.

2 Meanwhile, cook fish on heated lightly oiled flat plate (or large non-stick frying pan) until cooked as desired.

3 Combine sugar, vinegar, soy, chilli and ginger in large bowl. Place pineapple, capsicums and red onion in bowl with dressing; toss gently to combine. Divide mixture among serving plates; top with fish and green onion.

serves 4

per serving 25.7g carbohydrate; 4.8g total fat (1.4g saturated fat); 1393kJ (333 cal); 45.3g protein

carb tip Serve with steamed jasmine rice.

1 small pineapple (900g),
  chopped coarsely
1 large red capsicum (350g),
  chopped coarsely
1 medium green capsicum (200g),
  chopped coarsely
1 medium red onion (170g),
  sliced thinly
4 x 200g blue-eye fillets
2 tablespoons caster sugar
½ cup (125ml) white vinegar
2 tablespoons soy sauce
1 fresh long red chilli, seeded,
  sliced thinly
4cm piece fresh ginger (20g),
  grated
3 green onions, sliced thinly

vineleaf-wrapped ocean trout with braised fennel

PREPARATION TIME 20 MINUTES **COOKING TIME** 50 MINUTES

2 medium fennel bulbs (600g), untrimmed
1 large brown onion (200g), sliced thinly
2 cloves garlic, sliced thinly
1 tablespoon olive oil
¼ cup (60ml) orange juice
½ cup (125ml) chicken stock
¼ cup (60ml) dry white wine
8 large fresh grapevine leaves
4 x 200g ocean trout fillets
1 tablespoon finely grated orange rind
180g seedless white grapes

1 Preheat oven to moderate.
2 Reserve enough frond tips to make ¼ cup before trimming fennel bulbs. Slice fennel thinly then combine in large shallow baking dish with onion, garlic, oil, juice, stock and wine. Cook, covered, in moderate oven 30 minutes. Uncover, stir; cook, uncovered, in moderate oven about 20 minutes or until vegetables soften, stirring occasionally.
3 Meanwhile, dip vine leaves in medium saucepan of boiling water for 10 seconds; transfer immediately to medium bowl of iced water. Drain on absorbent paper. Slightly overlap two vine leaves, vein-sides up, on board; centre one fish fillet on leaves, top with a quarter of the rind and a quarter of the reserved frond tips. Fold leaves over to enclose fish. Repeat with remaining leaves, fish, rind and frond tips. Place vine-leaf parcels on oiled oven tray; bake in moderate oven about 15 minutes or until fish is cooked as desired.
4 Stir grapes into hot fennel mixture; stand, covered, 2 minutes before serving with fish.

serves 4
per serving 13.6g carbohydrate; 12.5g total fat (2.5g saturated fat);
1433kJ (342 cal); 41g protein
carb tip Serve with lentil, red onion and celery salad.

Available from early spring, fresh grapevine leaves can be found in most specialist greengrocers. Alternatively, you can purchase cryovac-packed-in-brine leaves from Middle-Eastern food stores; rinse and dry well before using.

red snapper parcels with caper anchovy salsa

PREPARATION TIME 30 MINUTES   **COOKING TIME** 15 MINUTES

A modern take on the traditional French method of cooking "en papillote" (in a sealed package), this recipe uses aluminium foil rather than parchment paper to enclose the ingredients. Cooking this way reduces the need for any added fat, plus mingles and intensifies the flavours of the parcel's contents.

1 Preheat oven to hot.

2 Combine garlic and fennel in small bowl.

3 Place fillets, skin-side down, on four separate squares of lightly oiled foil large enough to completely enclose fish. Top each fillet with equal amounts of the fennel mixture; top with one basil leaf each, drizzle each with 1 tablespoon of the wine. Gather corners of foil squares together above each fish; twist to enclose securely.

4 Place parcels on oven tray; bake in hot oven about 15 minutes or until fish is cooked as desired.

5 Meanwhile, make caper anchovy salsa.

6 Place remaining ingredients in medium bowl; toss gently to combine salad.

7 Unwrap parcels just before serving; divide fish, fennel-side up, among serving plates. Top with salsa; accompany with salad.

CAPER ANCHOVY SALSA Combine ingredients in small bowl.

serves 4
per serving 3.6g carbohydrate; 5.3g total fat (1.5g saturated fat); 1068kJ (255 cal); 43.9 protein
carb tip Serve with sliced steamed pontiac potatoes.

2 cloves garlic, crushed
1 baby fennel bulb (130g), sliced thinly
4 x 200g red snapper fillets
4 large fresh basil leaves
⅓ cup (80ml) dry white wine
¼ cup coarsely chopped fresh chives
⅓ cup loosely packed fresh tarragon leaves
⅓ cup loosely packed fresh basil leaves
½ cup loosely packed fresh chervil leaves
30g watercress, trimmed
1 tablespoon lemon juice
1 teaspoon olive oil

CAPER ANCHOVY SALSA
1 small red capsicum (150g), chopped finely
2 tablespoons finely chopped seeded kalamata olives
1 tablespoon drained baby capers, rinsed
8 drained anchovy fillets, chopped finely
¼ cup finely chopped fresh basil
1 tablespoon balsamic vinegar

barbecued squid and octopus salad

PREPARATION TIME 30 MINUTES (PLUS REFRIGERATION TIME) **COOKING TIME** 10 MINUTES

500g squid hoods

500g cleaned baby octopus

2 long green chillies,
   chopped finely

6 cloves garlic, crushed

500g asparagus, halved

500g yellow teardrop
   tomatoes, halved

200g cornichons, drained

1 large orange, sliced thickly

100g baby rocket leaves

ORANGE VINAIGRETTE

1 tablespoon olive oil

¼ cup (60ml) orange juice

1cm piece fresh ginger (5g),
   grated

1 teaspoon finely grated
   orange rind

2 tablespoons malt vinegar

1 Cut squid down centre to open out; score inside in diagonal pattern then cut into thick strips. Quarter octopus lengthways.

2 Combine squid and octopus in large bowl with chilli and garlic. Cover; refrigerate 3 hours or overnight.

3 Make orange vinaigrette.

4 Boil, steam or microwave asparagus until just tender; drain. Rinse under cold water; drain. Combine in large bowl with tomato, cornichons, orange and rocket.

5 Cook seafood, in batches, on heated lightly oiled grill plate (or grill or barbecue) until cooked through.

6 Add seafood and orange vinaigrette to bowl with asparagus salad; toss gently to combine.

ORANGE VINAIGRETTE Place ingredients in screw-top jar; shake well.

serves 4
per serving 13.6g carbohydrate; 7g total fat (1.2g saturated fat);
1086kJ (259 cal); 31.1g protein
carb tip Serve with steamed baby new potatoes.

cioppino

PREPARATION TIME 30 MINUTES **COOKING TIME** 40 MINUTES

1 Heat oil in large saucepan; cook onion, fennel and garlic, stirring, until onion softens. Add fresh tomato; cook, stirring, about 5 minutes or until pulpy. Stir in undrained crushed tomatoes, wine and stock; reduce heat, simmer, covered, 20 minutes.

2 Meanwhile, remove back shell from crabs; discard grey gills. Rinse crab; using sharp knife, chop each crab into four pieces. Shell and devein prawns, leaving tails intact. Chop fish into 2cm pieces.

3 Add clams to pan; simmer, covered, about 5 minutes or until clams open (discard any that do not). Add remaining seafood; cook, stirring occasionally, about 5 minutes or until seafood has changed in colour and is cooked as desired. Remove from heat; stir in herbs.

serves 4
per serving 13.1g carbohydrate; 6.4g total fat (1.4g saturated fat); 1476kJ (352 cal); 54.2g protein
carb tip Serve with a warm french bread stick.

2 teaspoons olive oil
1 medium brown onion (150g),
    chopped coarsely
1 baby fennel bulb (130g),
    trimmed, chopped coarsely
3 cloves garlic, crushed
6 medium tomatoes (1kg),
    chopped coarsely
425g can crushed tomatoes
½ cup (125ml) dry white wine
1½ cups (375ml) fish stock
2 cooked blue swimmer crabs (700g)
500g uncooked large king prawns
450g swordfish steaks
400g clams, rinsed
150g scallops
¼ cup coarsely chopped fresh basil
½ cup coarsely chopped fresh
    flat-leaf parsley

stir-fried octopus with basil

PREPARATION TIME 20 MINUTES **COOKING TIME** 10 MINUTES

1kg cleaned baby octopus

2 teaspoons peanut oil

2 teaspoons sesame oil

2 cloves garlic, crushed

2 fresh small red thai chillies, sliced thinly

2 large red capsicums (700g), sliced thinly

6 green onions, cut into 2cm lengths

¼ cup firmly packed fresh basil leaves

400g tat soi

2 tablespoons grated palm sugar

¼ cup (60ml) fish sauce

1 tablespoon kecap manis

¾ cup loosely packed fresh coriander leaves

1 Cut each octopus in half lengthways.

2 Heat peanut oil in wok; stir-fry octopus, in batches, until browned all over and tender. Cover to keep warm.

3 Heat sesame oil in same wok; stir-fry garlic, chilli and capsicum until capsicum is just tender. Return octopus to wok with onion, basil, tat soi, sugar and sauces; stir-fry until tat soi just wilts. Remove from heat; stir in coriander.

serves 4
per serving 14.5g carbohydrate; 7.7g total fat (1.3g saturated fat); 1229kJ (294 cal); 41.3g protein
carb tip Serve with steamed jasmine rice.

The mildly acrid baby bok choy, far smaller and more tender than bok choy, is perhaps the most popular of all the Asian greens so readily available in supermarkets everywhere today.

grilled kingfish with tamarind stir-fried vegetables

PREPARATION TIME 20 MINUTES **COOKING TIME** 10 MINUTES

2 teaspoons peanut oil

5cm piece fresh ginger (25g), cut into matchstick-sized pieces

2 cloves garlic, crushed

2 fresh long red chillies, chopped finely

1 medium red capsicum (200g), sliced thinly

¼ cup (60ml) chicken stock

2 tablespoons oyster sauce

1 tablespoon fish sauce

2 tablespoons grated palm sugar

1 tablespoon tamarind concentrate

250g baby bok choy, chopped coarsely

280g gai larn, chopped coarsely

8 green onions, cut into 3cm lengths

½ cup firmly packed fresh coriander leaves

4 x 200g kingfish steaks

1 Heat oil in wok; stir-fry ginger, garlic and chilli until fragrant. Add capsicum; stir-fry until capsicum is tender. Add stock, sauces, sugar and tamarind; bring to a boil. Boil 1 minute. Add bok choy, gai larn and onion; stir-fry until greens are just wilted. Remove from heat; stir in coriander.

2 Meanwhile, cook fish on heated lightly oiled grill plate (or grill or barbecue) about 5 minutes or until cooked as desired. Serve fish with vegetables.

serves 4

per serving 17.2g carbohydrate; 16g total fat (3.9g saturated fat); 1766kJ (421 cal); 52.1g protein

carb tip Serve with cellophane noodles.

salmon steaks with fennel salad

PREPARATION TIME 20 MINUTES **COOKING TIME** 5 MINUTES

1 Place vinegar, oil, sugar and mustard in screw-top jar; shake well.
2 Combine 1 tablespoon of the dressing with fish, finely chopped chives and finely chopped dill in medium bowl; toss fish to coat in mixture. Cook fish in heated lightly oiled large frying pan until cooked as desired.
3 Place remaining ingredients in large bowl with remaining dressing; toss gently to combine. Serve fish with salad.

serves 4
per serving 10.7g carbohydrate; 19g total fat (3.8g saturated fat); 1587kJ (379 cal); 41.1g protein
carb tip Serve with steamed pink fir apple potatoes.

2 tablespoons red wine vinegar
1 tablespoon olive oil
2 teaspoons sugar
2 teaspoons dijon mustard
4 x 200g salmon steaks
1 tablespoon finely chopped fresh chives
1 tablespoon finely chopped fresh dill
200g baby spinach leaves
2 medium apples (300g), sliced thinly
2 baby fennel bulbs (260g), trimmed, sliced thinly
1 lebanese cucumber (130g), seeded, sliced thinly
½ cup coarsely chopped fresh chives
¼ cup coarsely chopped fresh dill

steamed belgian mussels

PREPARATION TIME 30 MINUTES **COOKING TIME** 10 MINUTES

1.3kg black mussels
2 teaspoons olive oil
2 cloves garlic, crushed
3 shallots (75g), sliced thinly
2 trimmed celery stalks (200g),
   sliced thinly
2 large egg tomatoes (180g),
   chopped finely
½ cup (125ml) dry white wine
200g curly endive
½ cup loosely packed fresh
   flat-leaf parsley leaves
¼ cup coarsely chopped
   fresh chives
¼ cup (60ml) lemon juice

1 Scrub mussels; remove beards.
2 Heat oil in wok; stir-fry garlic, shallot and celery until shallot softens.
   Add tomato; stir-fry 30 seconds. Add wine; bring to a boil. Reduce
   heat; simmer, uncovered, until liquid reduces by half.
3 Add mussels; simmer, covered, about 5 minutes or until mussels
   open (discard any that do not).
4 Add remaining ingredients to wok; toss gently to combine. Serve
   mussels with broth in large serving bowls.

serves 4
per serving 6.8g carbohydrate; 3.8g total fat (0.7g saturated fat);
519kJ (124 cal); 9.9g protein
carb tip Serve with garlic bread.

grilled prawns with tropical fruits

PREPARATION TIME 15 MINUTES **COOKING TIME** 15 MINUTES

1 Make herb sauce.
2 Cook prawns on heated lightly oiled grill plate (or grill or barbecue) until changed in colour and cooked through.
3 Meanwhile, cook fruit on same grill plate until browned lightly.
4 Combine prawns and fruit in large bowl with mint and juice. Divide prawn mixture among serving bowls; drizzle with sauce.

HERB SAUCE Blend or process ingredients until combined.

serves 4
per serving 25g carbohydrate; 6.2g total fat (0.9g saturated fat); 1402kJ (335 cal); 43.7g protein
carb tip Serve with warm flour tortillas.

24 uncooked large
   king prawns (1.6kg)
¼ medium pineapple (300g),
   chopped coarsely
1 slightly firm large mango (600g),
   chopped coarsely
1 slightly firm large banana (230g),
   chopped coarsely
¼ cup loosely packed fresh
   mint leaves
2 tablespoons lime juice

HERB SAUCE
½ cup loosely packed fresh
   mint leaves
½ cup loosely packed fresh
   flat-leaf parsley leaves
1 clove garlic, quartered
2 tablespoons lime juice
1 tablespoon olive oil

tom yum goong

PREPARATION TIME 20 MINUTES **COOKING TIME** 20 MINUTES

1 Shell and devein prawns, reserve meat and shells separately. Discard heads.
2 Heat oil in large saucepan; cook shells, stirring, about 3 minutes or until deep orange in colour. Add lemon grass, garlic and ginger; cook, stirring, until fragrant.
3 Add the water and lime leaves, cover; bring to a boil. Reduce heat; simmer, uncovered, 10 minutes. Strain stock through muslin-lined sieve into large heatproof bowl; discard solids.
4 Return stock to same cleaned pan; bring to a boil. Reduce heat, add prawn meat; simmer, uncovered, until prawn meat is changed in colour. Remove from heat; stir in sauce and juice. Serve soup topped with chilli, onion, coriander and mint.

serves 4
per serving 2.1g carbohydrate; 5.5g total fat (1g saturated fat); 711kJ (170 cal); 27.1g protein
carb tip Serve with thin fresh rice noodles.

16 uncooked large
   king prawns (1.1kg)
1 tablespoon peanut oil
10cm stick (20g) fresh lemon
   grass, chopped coarsely
2 cloves garlic, quartered
3cm piece fresh ginger (15g),
   chopped coarsely
3 litres (12 cups) water
2 fresh kaffir lime leaves,
   chopped coarsely
2 tablespoons fish sauce
¼ cup (60ml) lime juice
2 fresh long red chillies,
   sliced thinly
3 green onions, sliced thinly
⅓ cup loosely packed fresh
   coriander leaves
¼ cup coarsely chopped
   fresh mint

grilled tuna with red cabbage salad

PREPARATION TIME 15 MINUTES **COOKING TIME** 10 MINUTES

1 tablespoon olive oil

1 medium red onion (170g),
sliced thinly

2 cups (160g) finely shredded
red cabbage

2 cups (160g) finely shredded
chinese cabbage

¼ cup (60ml) cider vinegar

1 large green apple (200g),
sliced thinly

1 cup loosely packed fresh
flat-leaf parsley leaves

4 x 200g tuna steaks

1 Heat oil in wok; stir-fry onion and cabbages 2 minutes. Add vinegar; bring
to a boil. Boil 1 minute. Remove from heat; stir in apple and parsley.

2 Meanwhile, cook fish on heated lightly oiled grill plate (or grill or barbecue)
until cooked as desired. Serve fish with warm cabbage salad.

serves 4

per serving 8.1g carbohydrate; 16.2g total fat (5.2g saturated fat);
1635kJ (391 cal); 52.5g protein

carb tip Serve with grilled kipfler potatoes.

poultry

pepper-roasted garlic and lemon chicken

PREPARATION TIME 35 MINUTES **COOKING TIME** I HOUR 50 MINUTES

1 Preheat oven to moderately hot.

2 Separate cloves from garlic bulb, leaving skin intact. Wash chicken under cold water; pat dry inside and out with absorbent paper. Coat chicken with cooking-oil spray; press combined salt and pepper onto skin and inside cavity. Place garlic and lemon inside cavity; tie legs together with kitchen string. Place chicken on small wire rack in large flameproof baking dish, pour the water in baking dish; roast, uncovered, in moderately hot oven 50 minutes.

3 Meanwhile, discard outer leaves from artichokes; cut tips from remaining leaves. Trim then peel stalks. Quarter artichokes lengthways; using teaspoon remove chokes. Cover artichoke with cold water in medium bowl, stir in the 2 tablespoons of lemon juice; soak artichoke until ready to cook.

4 Add drained artichoke, onion, fennel and leek to dish with chicken; coat with cooking-oil spray. Roast, uncovered, in moderately hot oven about 40 minutes or until vegetables are just tender.

5 Add tomatoes to dish; roast, uncovered, in moderately hot oven about 20 minutes or until tomatoes soften and chicken is cooked through. Place chicken on serving dish and vegetables in large bowl; cover to keep warm.

6 Stir wine and extra juice into dish with pan juices; bring to a boil. Boil 2 minutes then strain sauce over vegetables; toss gently to combine.

7 Discard garlic and lemon from cavity; serve chicken with vegetables.

2 bulbs garlic
2kg chicken
cooking-oil spray
2 teaspoons salt
2 tablespoons cracked
black pepper
1 medium lemon (140g),
cut into 8 wedges
1 cup (250ml) water
3 medium globe artichokes (660g)
2 tablespoons lemon juice
2 medium red onions (340g),
quartered
3 baby fennel bulbs (390g),
trimmed, halved
2 medium leeks (700g), halved
lengthways then quartered
250g cherry tomatoes
⅓ cup (80ml) dry white wine
¼ cup (60ml) lemon juice, extra

serves 4
per serving 19.8g carbohydrate; 42.3g total fat (12.9g saturated fat);
3026kJ (723 cal); 60.4g protein
carb tip Serve with roasted potato wedges.

cajun chicken with chunky salsa

PREPARATION TIME 20 MINUTES (PLUS REFRIGERATION TIME) **COOKING TIME** 20 MINUTES

4 single chicken breast fillets (680g)

1 teaspoon cracked black pepper

2 tablespoons finely chopped
   fresh oregano

2 teaspoons sweet paprika

1 teaspoon dried chilli flakes

2 cloves garlic, crushed

2 teaspoons olive oil

CHUNKY SALSA

2 medium tomatoes (300g),
   chopped coarsely

1 small red onion (100g),
   chopped coarsely

1 medium green capsicum (200g),
   chopped coarsely

2 tablespoons coarsely chopped
   fresh coriander

2 teaspoons olive oil

2 tablespoons lime juice

1 Place chicken in large bowl with combined remaining ingredients; toss chicken to coat in mixture. Cover; refrigerate 15 minutes.

2 Meanwhile, make chunky salsa.

3 Cook chicken in large lightly oiled non-stick frying pan until cooked through. Serve chicken with salsa.

CHUNKY SALSA Combine ingredients in medium bowl.

serves 4

per serving 3.9g carbohydrate; 8.7g total fat (1.7g saturated fat); 1085kJ (259 cal); 40.3g protein

carb tip Serve with warm corn tortillas.

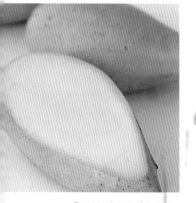

Sour and crunchy, green mangoes are just immature fruit that can be eaten as a vegetable in salads, curries and stir-fries. They will keep, wrapped in plastic, in the refrigerator up to two weeks.

spicy chicken legs
with mango salad

PREPARATION TIME 40 MINUTES **COOKING TIME** 30 MINUTES

2 teaspoons sesame oil
8 chicken drumsticks (1.2kg)
½ cup (125ml) chicken stock
2 teaspoons honey
2 tablespoons rice vinegar
1 teaspoon five-spice powder
6 cloves garlic, crushed
¼ cup (60ml) soy sauce
½ cup (125ml) water

MANGO SALAD
1 green mango (350g), sliced thinly
4 green onions, sliced thinly
1 cup loosely packed coriander leaves
150g snow peas, trimmed, halved
2 lebanese cucumbers (260g), seeded, sliced thinly
1½ cups (120g) bean sprouts

LIME AND VINEGAR DRESSING
¼ cup (60ml) lime juice
¼ cup (60ml) rice vinegar
2 teaspoons peanut oil

1 Heat oil in large deep frying pan; cook chicken, in batches, about 5 minutes or until browned all over.
2 Meanwhile, combine remaining ingredients in medium jug.
3 Return chicken to pan with stock mixture; bring to a boil. Reduce heat; simmer, covered, about 20 minutes or until chicken is cooked through.
4 Meanwhile, make mango salad. Make lime and vinegar dressing.
5 Pour dressing into salad; toss gently to combine. Divide chicken and salad among serving plates; drizzle remaining pan juices over chicken.

MANGO SALAD Combine ingredients in large bowl.
LIME AND VINEGAR DRESSING Place ingredients in screw-top jar; shake well.

serves 4
per serving 16.6g carbohydrate; 23.1g total fat (6.3g saturated fat); 1861kJ (445 cal); 41.5g protein
carb tip Serve with rice stick noodles tossed into salad.

neapolitan chicken parcels with rocket and red onion salad

PREPARATION TIME 20 MINUTES **COOKING TIME** 30 MINUTES

4 single chicken breast fillets (680g)

8 large fresh basil leaves

8 drained marinated artichoke heart quarters (100g)

⅔ cup (100g) semi-dried tomatoes

150g bocconcini cheese, sliced thinly

ROCKET AND RED ONION SALAD

1 tablespoon olive oil

2 tablespoons lemon juice

1 teaspoon dijon mustard

100g baby rocket leaves

½ cup loosely packed fresh basil leaves

1 medium red onion (170g), sliced thinly

1 tablespoon drained baby capers, rinsed

1 Using meat mallet, gently pound one chicken fillet between sheets of plastic wrap until 1cm in thickness. Place two of the large basil leaves on one side of chicken fillet; top leaves with two artichoke heart quarters, a quarter of the tomato and a quarter of the cheese. Fold chicken fillet over filling; tie with kitchen string to enclose securely. Repeat process with remaining chicken fillets, basil, artichoke, tomato and cheese.

2 Cook chicken parcels, uncovered, on heated oiled grill plate (or grill or barbecue) until browned both sides. Cover parcels with a flameproof lid or foil; cook about 15 minutes or until chicken is cooked through.

3 Meanwhile, make rocket and red onion salad. Serve chicken parcels with salad.

ROCKET AND RED ONION SALAD Whisk oil, juice and mustard in large bowl. Add remaining ingredients; toss gently to combine.

serves 4

per serving 12.4g carbohydrate; 16.3g total fat (5.7g saturated fat); 1786kJ (427 cal); 56.3g protein

carb tip Serve with penne, farfalle or shell pasta.

An artichoke heart, the tender meaty centre of the globe artichoke, is prized for its unique smoky, nutty flavour and vast adaptability to dishes from salads and appetisers to pizza toppings and stir-fries.

clay pot chicken

PREPARATION TIME 10 MINUTES (PLUS REFRIGERATION TIME) **COOKING TIME** 1 HOUR

1 Combine garlic, sauces, juice and lemon grass in large bowl, add chicken; toss chicken to coat in marinade. Cover; refrigerate 3 hours or overnight.

2 Preheat oven to moderate.

3 Place chicken mixture in clay pot or 2.5-litre (10-cup) ovenproof dish with brown onion, chilli and stock; mix gently to combine. Cook, covered, in moderate oven 45 minutes. Add mushroom, green onion and cabbage to dish; cook, covered, stirring occasionally, about 15 minutes or until chicken is cooked through.

serves 4

per serving 9.4g carbohydrate; 9.2g total fat (2.5g saturated fat); 1296kJ (310 cal); 46.6g protein

carb tip Serve with rinsed and drained wide rice noodles.

4 cloves garlic, crushed

1 tablespoon fish sauce

1 tablespoon soy sauce

1 tablespoon hoisin sauce

2 tablespoons lime juice

10cm stick (20g) fresh lemon grass, chopped finely

800g chicken thigh fillets, halved

1 large brown onion (200g), quartered

1 fresh long red chilli, sliced thinly

½ cup (125ml) chicken stock

100g fresh shiitake mushrooms, halved

4 green onions, cut into 4cm pieces

½ small cabbage (600g), cut into 6cm squares

chicken and vegetable soup

PREPARATION TIME 25 MINUTES **COOKING TIME** 20 MINUTES

1 Combine the water and stock in large saucepan; bring to a boil. Add carrot, celery and cauliflower; return to a boil. Reduce heat; simmer, covered, about 10 minutes or until just tender.

2 Add chicken and zucchini; cook, covered, about 5 minutes or until chicken is cooked through. Stir in snow peas and onion.

serves 4
per serving 10.2g carbohydrate; 4g total fat (1.3g saturated fat); 795kJ (190 cal); 28.2g protein
carb tip Add 1 large potato (300g), diced into 1cm pieces, to stock mixture with the first batch of vegetables.

2 cups (500ml) water
1.5 litres (6 cups) chicken stock
1 medium carrot (120g), diced into 1cm pieces
2 trimmed celery stalks (200g), sliced thinly
½ small cauliflower (500g), cut into florets
350g chicken breast fillets, sliced thinly
2 large zucchini (300g), diced into 1cm pieces
150g snow peas, trimmed, sliced thinly
3 green onions, sliced thinly

lemon pepper chicken with zucchini salad

PREPARATION TIME 20 MINUTES   **COOKING TIME** 40 MINUTES

1 tablespoon finely grated
  lemon rind
2 teaspoons cracked
  black pepper
⅓ cup (80ml) lemon juice
2 teaspoons olive oil
4 single chicken breast
  fillets (680g)
4 medium green zucchini (480g)
4 medium yellow zucchini (480g)
1 clove garlic, crushed
4 green onions, chopped finely
1 cup coarsely chopped fresh
  flat-leaf parsley
¼ cup coarsely chopped
  fresh tarragon

1 Combine rind, pepper, 1 tablespoon of the juice and half of the oil in large bowl, add chicken; toss chicken to coat in marinade. Cover; refrigerate until required.

2 Peel zucchini randomly; slice into thin strips diagonally. Cook zucchini slices, in batches, on heated lightly oiled grill plate (or grill or barbecue) until browned lightly and tender.

3 Cook chicken on same grill plate until cooked through.

4 Meanwhile, whisk remaining juice and remaining oil with garlic in large bowl. Place zucchini, onion and herbs in bowl with dressing; toss gently to combine.

5 Serve chicken with zucchini salad.

serves 4
per serving 4.1g carbohydrate; 7.5g total fat (1.5g saturated fat); 1198kJ (286 cal); 48.9g protein
carb tip Serve with steamed chats.

Before threading the ingredients onto skewers, soak twelve 25cm-long bamboo skewers in cold water for at least an hour to prevent them from splintering or scorching.

chicken, lemon and artichoke skewers

PREPARATION TIME 20 MINUTES **COOKING TIME** 15 MINUTES

3 medium lemons (420g)
3 small red onions (300g)
500g chicken breast fillets, diced into 3cm pieces
400g can marinated quartered artichoke hearts, drained
300g mushrooms
100g baby rocket leaves
2 tablespoons drained baby capers, rinsed

LEMON DRESSING
1 tablespoon lemon juice
2 cloves garlic, crushed
½ teaspoon mild english mustard
1 tablespoon white wine vinegar
1 tablespoon olive oil

1 Make lemon dressing.
2 Cut each lemon into eight wedges; cut two of the onions into six wedges. Thread lemon and onion wedges, chicken, artichokes and mushrooms, alternately, onto skewers.
3 Place skewers in shallow dish; brush with half of the dressing. Cook skewers on heated lightly oiled grill plate (or grill or barbecue) until cooked through.
4 Meanwhile, slice remaining onion thinly, place in large bowl with rocket, capers and remaining dressing; toss gently to combine. Divide salad among serving plates; top each with three skewers.

LEMON DRESSING Place ingredients in screw-top jar; shake well.

serves 4
per serving 7.9g carbohydrate; 8.3g total fat (1.4g saturated fat); 1057kJ (252 cal); 34.3g protein
carb tip Serve with cooked barley or brown rice.

poached chicken with ruby grapefruit salad

PREPARATION TIME 40 MINUTES **COOKING TIME** 10 MINUTES

1 Combine the water and stock in large frying pan; bring to a boil. Add chicken; return to a boil. Reduce heat; simmer, covered, about 10 minutes or until cooked through. Cool chicken in poaching liquid 10 minutes. Remove chicken from pan; discard poaching liquid. Slice chicken thinly.

2 Meanwhile, halve red onion; cut each half into thin wedges.

3 Segment peeled grapefruit over large bowl to catch juice; add grapefruit segments to bowl with chicken, onions, chilli, coriander, nuts and spinach.

4 Place remaining ingredients in small jug; whisk until sugar dissolves. Pour dressing over salad; toss gently to combine.

serves 4
per serving 7g carbohydrate; 8g total fat (1.5g saturated fat); 1066kJ (255 cal); 37.8g protein
carb tip Rice stick noodles can be used as a bed for this salad.

If pomelos are available in your area, they can be substituted for the grapefruit.

2½ cups (625ml) water
2½ cups (625ml) chicken stock
700g chicken breast fillets
1 small red onion (100g)
4 ruby red grapefruits (2kg)
4 green onions, sliced thinly
2 fresh small red thai chillies, sliced thinly
1 cup coarsely chopped fresh coriander
¼ cup (35g) toasted unsalted peanuts
100g baby spinach leaves
2 cloves garlic, crushed
1 tablespoon grated palm sugar
1 tablespoon lime juice
1 tablespoon soy sauce

asian chicken broth

PREPARATION TIME 30 MINUTES **COOKING TIME** 20 MINUTES

1 litre (4 cups) water

1 litre (4 cups) chicken stock

10cm stick (20g) fresh lemon
   grass, chopped finely

4cm piece fresh ginger (20g),
   sliced thinly

2 fresh small red thai chillies,
   sliced thinly

2 tablespoons soy sauce

1 tablespoon lime juice

1 tablespoon fish sauce

500g choy sum,
   chopped coarsely

3 green onions, sliced thinly

⅓ cup loosely packed fresh
   coriander leaves

CHICKEN DUMPLINGS

400g chicken mince

1 tablespoon finely chopped
   fresh coriander

2 cloves garlic, crushed

1 Combine the water, stock, lemon grass, ginger, chilli and soy sauce in
   large saucepan: bring to a boil. Reduce heat; simmer, uncovered, about
   5 minutes.

2 Meanwhile, make chicken dumplings.

3 Add chicken dumplings to simmering broth; simmer, covered, about
   5 minutes or until dumplings are cooked through.

4 Add juice, fish sauce, choy sum and onion to broth; cook, uncovered, about
   2 minutes or until choy sum just wilts. Stir in coriander just before serving.

CHICKEN DUMPLINGS Using hand, combine mince, coriander and garlic in
medium bowl. Using hands, roll level tablespoons of the mixture into balls.

serves 4

per serving 4.3g carbohydrate; 9.4g total fat (2.9g saturated fat);
848kJ (202 cal); 24.6g protein

carb tip Add bean thread noodles to broth with the dumplings.

Used in Middle-Eastern cooking for centuries, sumac now adds its tart, lemony flavour to dips, dressings and barbecued meat, seafood and poultry in restaurant and domestic kitchens all over the country.

You will need to soak eight 25cm bamboo skewers in water for at least an hour before using to prevent them from splintering or scorching.

sumac and paprika-spiced chicken with herb salad

PREPARATION TIME 20 MINUTES **COOKING TIME** 15 MINUTES

800g chicken tenderloins
2 cloves garlic, crushed
2 teaspoons sweet paprika
2 tablespoons sumac
2 teaspoons finely chopped fresh oregano
2 tablespoons water
1 teaspoon vegetable oil
2½ cups coarsely chopped fresh flat-leaf parsley
1 cup coarsely chopped fresh coriander
½ cup coarsely chopped fresh mint
4 medium tomatoes (600g), chopped coarsely
1 medium red onion (170g), chopped coarsely
⅓ cup (80ml) lemon juice
1 tablespoon olive oil

1 Thread chicken onto skewers. Using fingers, rub combined garlic, paprika, sumac, oregano, the water and vegetable oil all over chicken. Cook chicken on heated lightly oiled grill plate (or grill or barbecue) until cooked through.
2 Meanwhile, place herbs, tomato and onion in medium bowl with juice and olive oil; toss gently to combine. Serve chicken skewers with herb salad.

serves 4
per serving 6.6g carbohydrate; 10.7g total fat (2g saturated fat); 1367kJ (327 cal); 48.8g protein
carb tip Serve with warm pitta bread.

chicken tikka with raita

PREPARATION TIME 20 MINUTES **COOKING TIME** 20 MINUTES

1 Cook chicken, in batches, in large deep lightly oiled frying pan until browned all over.

2 Cook onion and capsicum in same pan, stirring, until onion softens. Add chilli and paste; cook, stirring, until fragrant. Return chicken to pan with cream; bring to a boil. Reduce heat; simmer, uncovered, about 5 minutes or until chicken is cooked through. Remove from heat; stir in tomato and coriander.

3 Meanwhile, make raita.

4 Serve chicken on sprouts topped with raita.

RAITA Combine ingredients in small bowl.

serves 4
per serving 16g carbohydrate; 38.8g total fat (15.9g saturated fat); 2532kJ (605 cal); 48.3g protein
carb tip Serve with steamed basmati rice.

800g chicken thigh fillets, sliced thickly
1 medium brown onion (150g), cut into wedges
1 large red capsicum (350g), chopped coarsely
2 long green chillies, sliced thinly
⅓ cup (100g) tikka curry paste
300ml light cream
250g cherry tomatoes, halved
¾ cup loosely packed fresh coriander leaves
3 cups (240g) bean sprouts

RAITA
200g low-fat yogurt
1 lebanese cucumber (130g), seeded, chopped finely
1 tablespoon finely chopped fresh mint

braised spatchcocks with spinach

PREPARATION TIME 30 MINUTES **COOKING TIME** 40 MINUTES

3 x 500g spatchcocks
1 medium leek (350g),
   chopped coarsely
2 cloves garlic, crushed
1 medium brown onion (150g),
   chopped coarsely
4 bacon rashers (280g), rind
   removed, chopped finely
½ cup (125ml) dry white wine
1 cup (250ml) chicken stock
2 bay leaves
300g brussels sprouts, halved
500g spinach, trimmed,
   chopped coarsely
½ cup coarsely chopped
   fresh mint

1 Cut along both sides of spatchcocks' backbones; discard backbones. Cut each spatchcock into four pieces. Rinse under cold water; pat dry with absorbent paper.

2 Cook spatchcock, in batches, in large lightly oiled saucepan until browned lightly both sides. Cook leek, garlic, onion and bacon in same pan, stirring, about 5 minutes or until leek softens. Add wine, stock and bay leaves; bring to a boil. Return spatchcocks with any juices to pan, reduce heat; simmer, uncovered, about 20 minutes or until liquid has almost evaporated. Discard bay leaves. Remove spatchcock from pan; cover to keep warm.

3 Add sprouts; simmer, uncovered, about 3 minutes or until tender. Stir in spinach and mint; cook until spinach just wilts. Serve spatchcock with sprouts and spinach mixture.

serves 4
per serving 7.4g carbohydrate; 30.1g total fat (9.6g saturated fat); 2304kJ (551 cal); 57.6g protein
carb tip Serve with mashed potatoes.

osso buco

PREPARATION TIME 30 MINUTES **COOKING TIME** 2 HOURS 30 MINUTES

An Italian gremolata is traditionally a blend of finely chopped lemon rind, parsley and garlic. Sprinkled over osso buco just before serving warms the gremolata, enlivening it just enough to send a sharp aromatic message to the diner's tastebuds.

1 tablespoon olive oil
8 pieces veal osso buco (2kg)
1 medium brown onion (150g), chopped coarsely
2 cloves garlic, crushed
1 trimmed celery stalk (100g), chopped coarsely
1 large carrot (180g), chopped coarsely
2 tablespoons tomato paste
½ cup (125ml) dry white wine
1 cup (250ml) beef stock
1 cup (250ml) water
400g can crushed tomatoes
1 teaspoon fresh rosemary leaves
1 medium eggplant (300g), chopped coarsely
1 medium green capsicum (200g), chopped coarsely
1 medium yellow capsicum (200g), chopped coarsely

GREMOLATA
2 teaspoons finely grated lemon rind
¼ cup finely chopped fresh flat-leaf parsley
1 tablespoon finely chopped fresh rosemary
1 clove garlic, chopped finely

Ask your butcher to cut the veal shin into fairly thick (about 3cm to 4cm) pieces for you.

1 Heat half of the oil in large saucepan; cook veal, in batches, until browned all over.
2 Heat remaining oil in same dish; cook onion, garlic, celery and carrot, stirring, until vegetables soften. Stir in tomato paste, wine, stock, the water, undrained tomatoes and rosemary; bring to a boil.
3 Return veal to dish, fitting pieces upright and tightly together in single layer; return to a boil. Reduce heat; simmer, covered, 1½ hours. Add eggplant; cook, uncovered, 15 minutes, stirring occasionally. Add capsicums; cook, uncovered, about 15 minutes or until vegetables are tender.
4 Meanwhile, make gremolata.
5 Remove veal and vegetables from dish; cover to keep warm. Bring sauce to a boil; boil, uncovered, about 10 minutes or until sauce thickens slightly.
6 Divide veal and vegetables among serving plates; top with sauce, sprinkle with gremolata.

GREMOLATA Combine ingredients in small bowl.

serves 4
per serving 11.9g carbohydrate; 6.6g total fat (1g saturated fat);
1796kJ (429 cal); 74.2g protein
carb tip Serve with creamy polenta flavoured with parmesan cheese.

marjoram and lemon-grilled veal chops with greek salad

PREPARATION TIME 25 MINUTES (PLUS REFRIGERATION TIME)
COOKING TIME 10 MINUTES

1 teaspoon finely grated lemon rind
¼ cup (60ml) lemon juice
1 tablespoon finely chopped fresh marjoram
2 teaspoons olive oil
4 x 200g veal chops

GREEK SALAD
¾ cup (120g) seeded kalamata olives
200g fetta cheese, chopped coarsely
6 large egg tomatoes (540g), seeded, chopped coarsely
1 medium red capsicum (200g), chopped coarsely
2 lebanese cucumbers (260g), seeded, sliced thinly
2 trimmed celery stalks (200g), sliced thinly
1 tablespoon fresh marjoram leaves

LEMON DRESSING
1 clove garlic, crushed
⅓ cup (80ml) lemon juice
2 teaspoons olive oil

An olive pipper is a great kitchen tool: it can pop the seeds out of cherries as well as olives, plus it can be used to perform the reverse task of stuffing olives with bits of anchovy, fetta or sun-dried tomato.

1 Combine rind, juice, marjoram and oil in large bowl, add veal; toss veal to coat in marinade. Cover; refrigerate 1 hour.
2 Meanwhile, make greek salad. Make lemon dressing.
3 Cook veal on heated lightly oiled grill plate (or grill or barbecue) until cooked as desired.
4 Pour dressing over salad; toss gently to combine. Serve veal with salad.

GREEK SALAD Combine ingredients in large bowl.
LEMON DRESSING Place ingredients in screw-top jar; shake well.

serves 4
per serving 14.8g carbohydrate; 19.9g total fat (9.3g saturated fat); 1697kJ (405 cal); 40.7g protein
carb tip Serve with a sourdough baguette.

The Thai pickled green peppercorns used here are extremely pungent, having a fresh "green" flavour that the dried ones lack. They are available, canned in brine, from most Asian food shops. Conventional green peppercorns can be substituted, but the flavour will not be as intense.

crying tiger

PREPARATION TIME 25 MINUTES (PLUS REFRIGERATION TIME)
COOKING TIME 10 MINUTES

600g piece beef eye fillet
1 teaspoon tamarind concentrate
2 cloves garlic, crushed
2 teaspoons pickled green peppercorns, crushed
2 tablespoons fish sauce
2 tablespoons soy sauce
10cm stick (20g) fresh lemon grass, chopped finely
2 fresh small red thai chillies, chopped finely
1 medium red capsicum (200g), sliced thickly
1 cup (80g) finely shredded chinese cabbage
6 trimmed red radishes (90g), sliced thickly
4 green onions, cut into 3cm pieces

CRYING TIGER SAUCE
2 teaspoons tamarind concentrate
¼ cup (60ml) fish sauce
¼ cup (60ml) lime juice
2 teaspoons grated palm sugar
1 fresh small red thai chilli, chopped finely
1 green onion, sliced thinly
2 teaspoons finely chopped fresh coriander

1 Halve beef lengthways. Combine tamarind, garlic, pepper, sauces, lemon grass and chilli in large bowl, add beef; toss beef to coat in marinade. Cover; refrigerate 3 hours or overnight.
2 Cook drained beef on heated oiled grill plate (or grill or barbecue) until cooked as desired. Cover beef; stand 10 minutes then slice thinly.
3 Meanwhile, make crying tiger sauce.
4 Place beef on serving platter with capsicum, cabbage, radish and onion; serve with crying tiger sauce.

CRYING TIGER SAUCE Combine ingredients in small bowl; whisk until sugar dissolves.

serves 4
per serving 6.6g carbohydrate; 7.8g total fat (2.9g saturated fat); 1074kJ (256 cal); 38.7g protein
carb tip Serve with warm flour tortillas.

eggplant bolognese bake

PREPARATION TIME 30 MINUTES **COOKING TIME** 1 HOUR 10 MINUTES

2 medium eggplants (600g)
200g baby spinach leaves
150g ricotta
1 egg white
½ cup (50g) coarsely grated
   mozzarella cheese
⅓ cup (25g) coarsely grated
   parmesan cheese

BOLOGNESE SAUCE

2 teaspoons olive oil
1 large brown onion (200g),
   chopped coarsely
1 small red capsicum (150g),
   chopped coarsely
1 small green capsicum (150g),
   chopped coarsely
2 cloves garlic, crushed
250g beef mince
1 large egg tomato (90g),
   chopped coarsely
1 tablespoon tomato paste
½ cup (125ml) dry red wine
400g can crushed tomatoes
2 tablespoons coarsely
   chopped fresh basil
1 tablespoon coarsely chopped
   fresh oregano

ROCKET SALAD

100g baby rocket leaves
½ cup loosely packed fresh
   basil leaves
1 tablespoon balsamic vinegar
1 teaspoon olive oil

1 Make bolognese sauce.
2 Meanwhile, cut eggplants into 2mm slices; cook on heated lightly oiled grill plate (or grill or barbecue) until just tender.
3 Preheat oven to moderate.
4 Boil, steam or microwave spinach until wilted; drain. Cool 10 minutes; using hands, squeeze as much liquid as possible from spinach. Combine spinach, ricotta and egg white in medium bowl.
5 Spread 1 cup of the sauce over base of shallow 2-litre (8-cup) ovenproof dish. Top with half of the eggplant, then half of the spinach mixture, then another cup of sauce, remaining eggplant and remaining spinach mixture. Spread remaining sauce over the top then sprinkle with combined cheeses. Bake, uncovered, in moderate oven about 20 minutes or until top browns lightly. Stand 10 minutes.
6 Meanwhile, make rocket salad.
7 Divide bolognese bake among serving plates; serve with rocket salad.

BOLOGNESE SAUCE Heat oil in medium frying pan; cook onion, capsicums and garlic, stirring, until onion softens. Add beef to pan; cook, stirring, until beef changes colour. Add chopped tomato and tomato paste; cook, stirring, 3 minutes. Stir in wine and undrained tomatoes; bring to a boil. Reduce heat; simmer, uncovered, about 25 minutes or until sauce thickens. Remove from heat; stir in herbs.
ROCKET SALAD Combine ingredients in medium bowl.

serves 4
per serving 13.4g carbohydrate; 20.3g total fat (9.2g saturated fat);
1563kJ (373 cal); 29.1g protein
carb tip Serve with penne pasta or elbow macaroni.

Also known as chinese black, forest or golden oak mushrooms, shiitake are used as a meat substitute in many Asian vegetarian dishes. Although they are cultivated mushrooms, shiitake have the earthy flavour of wild mushrooms.

hoisin beef stir-fry

PREPARATION TIME 20 MINUTES (PLUS REFRIGERATION TIME) **COOKING TIME** 15 MINUTES

1 teaspoon sesame oil
1 teaspoon cracked black pepper
2 green onions, chopped finely
1 fresh small red thai chilli, chopped finely
2 cloves garlic, crushed
3cm piece fresh ginger (15g), grated
⅓ cup (80ml) chinese rice wine
⅓ cup (80ml) soy sauce
800g beef strips
1 tablespoon peanut oil
1 medium brown onion (150g), sliced thinly
1 medium red capsicum (200g), sliced thinly
100g fresh shiitake mushrooms, trimmed, sliced thinly
500g choy sum, halved horizontally
¼ cup (60ml) water
¼ cup (60ml) hoisin sauce
4 green onions, sliced thinly

1 Combine sesame oil, pepper, finely chopped green onion, chilli, garlic, ginger, half of the wine and half of the soy sauce in large bowl, add beef; toss beef to coat in marinade. Cover; refrigerate 3 hours or overnight.
2 Heat half of the peanut oil in wok; cook beef mixture, in batches, until beef is browned.
3 Heat remaining peanut oil in same wok; stir-fry brown onion and capsicum until almost tender. Add mushroom, choy sum stalks, the water, hoisin, remaining wine and remaining soy sauce; stir-fry about 5 minutes or until vegetables are tender.
4 Return beef to wok with choy sum leaves; stir-fry until choy sum leaves just wilt.
5 Divide stir-fry among serving bowls; top with sliced green onion.

serves 4
per serving 13.7g carbohydrate; 16.6g total fat (5.3g saturated fat);
1730kJ (413 cal); 46.8g protein
carb tip Serve with steamed jasmine rice.

spicy char-grilled beef and citrus salad

PREPARATION TIME 25 MINUTES (PLUS REFRIGERATION TIME)
COOKING TIME 10 MINUTES

Mesclun, sometimes sold as spring salad mix, is a commercial assortment of young green leaves, and will usually include some or all of the following: rocket, mizuna, baby spinach, curly endive, oak leaf, radicchio and mignonette.

2 cloves garlic, crushed
⅓ cup (80ml) orange juice
¼ cup (60ml) lime juice
1 tablespoon soy sauce
1 teaspoon dried chilli flakes
1 tablespoon white wine vinegar
800g beef rump steak
250g asparagus, trimmed
1 medium orange (240g)
150g mesclun
250g witlof, chopped coarsely
½ cup coarsely chopped fresh basil
3 shallots (75g), sliced thinly
250g cherry tomatoes, halved

ORANGE DRESSING
⅓ cup (80ml) lime juice
1 tablespoon orange juice
2 teaspoons olive oil

1 Combine garlic, juices, sauce, chilli and vinegar in large bowl, add beef; toss beef to coat in marinade. Cover; refrigerate 3 hours or overnight.
2 Cook beef mixture on heated oiled grill plate (or grill or barbecue) until cooked as desired. Cover beef; stand 10 minutes then slice thinly.
3 Meanwhile, cook asparagus on same grill plate until just tender; cut each spear into thirds.
4 Make orange dressing.
5 Segment orange over large bowl, add beef, asparagus and dressing with remaining ingredients; toss gently to combine.

ORANGE DRESSING Place ingredients in screw-top jar; shake well.

You need two oranges and four limes for this recipe.

serves 4
per serving 10.1g carbohydrate; 12.1g total fat (4.8g saturated fat); 1454kJ (347 cal); 47.6g protein
carb tip Serve with grilled polenta triangles.

Baby eggplants and baby fennel, like most other baby vegetables, are sweeter, more tender and less coarse than their adult counterparts. This tends to make them the most desirable for use in recipes that require little treatment or cooking.

basil and oregano steak with char-grilled vegetables

PREPARATION TIME 20 MINUTES **COOKING TIME** 30 MINUTES

2 teaspoons finely chopped fresh oregano
¼ cup finely chopped fresh basil
1 tablespoon finely grated lemon rind
2 tablespoons lemon juice
4 drained anchovy fillets, chopped finely
4 x 200g beef sirloin steaks
2 baby fennel bulbs (260g), quartered
3 small zucchini (270g), chopped coarsely
1 large red capsicum (350g), sliced thickly
200g portobello mushrooms, sliced thickly
4 baby eggplants (240g), chopped coarsely
2 small red onions (200g), sliced thickly
2 teaspoons olive oil
¼ cup (60ml) lemon juice
2 tablespoons fresh oregano leaves

1 Combine chopped oregano, basil, rind, the 2 tablespoons of lemon juice and anchovy in large bowl, add beef; toss beef to coat in marinade. Cover; refrigerate until required.
2 Meanwhile, combine fennel, zucchini, capsicum, mushroom, eggplant, onion and oil in large bowl; cook vegetables, in batches, on heated lightly oiled grill plate (or grill or barbecue) until just tender. Add juice and oregano leaves to bowl with vegetables; toss gently to combine. Cover to keep warm.
3 Cook beef mixture on same grill plate until cooked as desired; serve with vegetables.

serves 4
per serving 9.6g carbohydrate; 21.3g total fat (8.6g saturated fat);
1779kJ (425 cal); 47.8g protein
carb tip Serve with char-grilled fresh corn cobs.

vietnamese beef, chicken and tofu soup

PREPARATION TIME 20 MINUTES **COOKING TIME** 1 HOUR 5 MINUTES

1 Combine the water, beef, star anise, galangal and sauces in large saucepan; bring to a boil. Reduce heat; simmer, covered, 30 minutes. Uncover; simmer, 20 minutes. Add chicken; simmer, uncovered, 10 minutes.
2 Combine sprouts, coriander, onion, chilli and juice in medium bowl.
3 Remove beef and chicken from pan; reserve stock. Discard fat and sinew from beef; slice thinly. Slice chicken thinly. Return beef and chicken to pan; reheat soup.
4 Divide tofu among serving bowls; ladle hot soup over tofu, sprinkle with sprout mixture. Serve with lime wedges and extra chilli, if desired.

serves 4
per serving 3.6g carbohydrate; 18.8g total fat (6.5g saturated fat); 1410kJ (337 cal); 37.6g protein
carb tip Serve with bean thread vermicelli.

3 litres (12 cups) water
500g gravy beef
1 star anise
2.5cm piece fresh galangal (45g), halved
¼ cup (60ml) soy sauce
2 tablespoons fish sauce
340g chicken breast fillets
1½ cups (120g) bean sprouts
1 cup loosely packed fresh coriander leaves
4 green onions, sliced thinly
2 fresh small red thai chillies, sliced thinly
⅓ cup (80ml) lime juice
300g firm tofu, diced into 2cm pieces

beef and mushrooms in red wine sauce

PREPARATION TIME 20 MINUTES **COOKING TIME** 2 HOURS

4 bacon rashers (280g), rind
  removed, sliced thinly
800g gravy beef, diced into
  2cm pieces
1 cup (250ml) dry red wine
2 tablespoons tomato paste
1½ cups (375ml) beef stock
1 cup (250ml) water
2 cloves garlic, crushed
1 teaspoon fresh thyme leaves
1 tablespoon vegetable oil
16 shallots (400g)
400g mushrooms
500g broccoli, cut into florets
½ cup coarsely chopped
  fresh flat-leaf parsley

1 Cook bacon in large heavy-based saucepan, stirring, until browned; drain on absorbent paper. Cook beef, in batches, in same pan, stirring until browned all over.

2 Return bacon and beef to pan with wine, paste, stock, the water, garlic and thyme; bring to a boil. Reduce heat; simmer, covered, 1½ hours.

3 Meanwhile, heat oil in large frying pan, cook shallots, stirring occasionally, until browned and starting to soften. Add mushrooms; cook, stirring, about 10 minutes or until mushrooms soften.

4 Remove beef from pan; cover to keep warm. Bring sauce in pan to a boil. Reduce heat; simmer, uncovered, until reduced by half.

5 Meanwhile, boil, steam or microwave broccoli until tender; drain.

6 Return beef to pan with shallot mixture; stir gently until heated through. Remove from heat; stir in parsley. Serve beef with broccoli.

serves 4
per serving 8.7g carbohydrate; 30.8g total fat (11.1g saturated fat); 2621kJ (626 cal); 67.7g protein
carb tip Serve with polenta made with chopped parsley and cream.

lamb

These small, grape-shaped, red tomatoes are similar in texture and colour to cherry tomatoes, but have a richer, fuller and slightly less acidic flavour, making them perfect for adding to salads or crudité platters.

lemon and garlic cutlets with fetta salad

PREPARATION TIME 15 MINUTES **COOKING TIME** 15 MINUTES

1 tablespoon finely grated lemon rind
2 tablespoons lemon juice
2 cloves garlic, crushed
12 french-trimmed lamb cutlets (600g)
160g snow pea sprouts, trimmed
250g grape tomatoes, halved
1 cup coarsely chopped fresh mint
1 cup coarsely chopped fresh basil
200g fetta cheese, crumbled
½ cup (75g) seeded kalamata olives

LEMON DRESSING
¼ cup (60ml) lemon juice
2 teaspoons olive oil
1 teaspoon dijon mustard

1 Combine rind, juice and garlic in large bowl, add lamb; toss lamb to coat in marinade.
2 Make lemon dressing.
3 Cook lamb, in batches, on heated oiled grill plate (or grill or barbecue) until cooked as desired.
4 Place remaining ingredients and half of the dressing in medium bowl; toss gently to combine.
5 Serve salad with lamb; drizzle lamb with remaining dressing.

LEMON DRESSING Place ingredients in screw-top jar; shake well.

serves 4
per serving 14.8g carbohydrate; 19.9g total fat (10.4g saturated fat); 1515kJ (362 cal); 30.3g protein
carb tip Toss cooked short pasta through salad.

lamb shanks in five-spice, tamarind and ginger

PREPARATION TIME 20 MINUTES **COOKING TIME** 2 HOURS 10 MINUTES

2 teaspoons five-spice powder

1 teaspoon dried chilli flakes

1 cinnamon stick

2 star anise

¼ cup (60ml) soy sauce

½ cup (125ml) chinese rice wine

2 tablespoons tamarind
concentrate

2 tablespoons brown sugar

8cm piece fresh ginger (40g),
grated

2 cloves garlic, chopped coarsely

1¼ cups (310ml) water

8 french-trimmed
lamb shanks (1.6kg)

500g choy sum, chopped
into 10cm lengths

350g gai larn, trimmed

1 Preheat oven to moderate.

2 Dry-fry five-spice, chilli, cinnamon and star anise in small heated frying pan, stirring, until fragrant. Combine spices with sauce, wine, tamarind, sugar, ginger, garlic and the water in medium jug.

3 Place lamb, in single layer, in large shallow baking dish; drizzle with spice mixture. Bake, covered, in moderate oven, turning lamb occasionally, about 2 hours or until meat is almost falling off the bone. Remove lamb from dish; cover to keep warm. Skim away excess fat; strain sauce into small saucepan.

4 Boil, steam or microwave choy sum and gai larn, separately, until tender; drain.

5 Bring sauce to a boil; boil, uncovered, 2 minutes. Divide vegetables among serving plates; serve with lamb, drizzle with sauce.

serves 4

per serving 10.8g carbohydrate; 20.2g total fat (9g saturated fat); 1912kJ (456 cal); 50.5 protein

carb tip Serve with steamed basmati rice.

lamb shank soup

PREPARATION TIME 30 MINUTES **COOKING TIME** 2 HOURS 30 MINUTES (PLUS COOLING AND REFRIGERATION TIME)

1 Heat large lightly oiled saucepan; cook lamb, in batches, until browned. Cook onion, celery, capsicum and garlic in same pan, stirring, about 5 minutes or until onion softens. Return lamb to pan with the water; bring to a boil. Reduce heat; simmer, covered, 1¾ hours.

2 Remove soup mixture from heat; when lamb is cool enough to handle, remove meat from bones then chop coarsely. Refrigerate cooled soup and meat, covered separately, overnight.

3 Discard fat from surface of soup mixture. Place soup mixture and meat in large saucepan; bring to a boil. Reduce heat; simmer, covered, 30 minutes. Add silverbeet and juice; simmer, uncovered, until silverbeet just wilts.

serves 4
per serving 7.5g carbohydrate; 20.8g total fat (9.1g saturated fat); 1728kJ (413 cal); 48.1g protein
carb tip Serve with crusty bread.

8 french-trimmed
 lamb shanks (1.6kg)
1 medium brown onion (150g),
 chopped finely
2 trimmed celery stalks (200g),
 sliced thinly
2 medium red capsicums (400g),
 chopped coarsely
2 cloves garlic, crushed
2 litres (8 cups) water
400g silverbeet, trimmed,
 chopped finely
⅓ cup (80ml) lemon juice

raan with baby beans and spiced yogurt

PREPARATION TIME 35 MINUTES (PLUS REFRIGERATION TIME) **COOKING TIME** 20 MINUTES

2 teaspoons coriander seeds

1 teaspoon cumin seeds

5 cardamom pods, bruised

1 teaspoon chilli powder

1 teaspoon ground turmeric

1 cinnamon stick

2 cloves

2 star anise

1 medium brown onion (150g), chopped coarsely

4 cloves garlic, quartered

2cm piece fresh ginger (10g), chopped coarsely

¼ cup (40g) blanched almonds

½ cup (140g) low-fat yogurt

2 tablespoons lemon juice

1.2kg butterflied leg of lamb, trimmed

GREEN BEAN SALAD

500g green beans, halved

3 shallots (75g), sliced thinly

⅓ cup (45g) toasted slivered almonds

¼ cup (40g) sultanas

⅓ cup loosely packed fresh mint leaves

1 teaspoon extra virgin olive oil

⅓ cup (80ml) lemon juice

SPICED YOGURT

1 cup (280g) low-fat yogurt

¼ cup finely chopped fresh mint

1 clove garlic, crushed

¼ teaspoon ground cumin

¼ teaspoon ground coriander

1 Dry-fry seeds, cardamom, chilli, turmeric, cinnamon, cloves and star anise in small heated frying pan, stirring, about 2 minutes or until fragrant. Blend or process spices with onion, garlic, ginger, nuts, yogurt and juice until mixture forms a paste.

2 Pierce lamb all over with sharp knife; place on metal rack in large shallow baking dish. Spread paste over lamb, pressing firmly into cuts. Cover, refrigerate 3 hours or overnight.

3 Cook lamb on heated oiled grill plate (or grill or barbecue), covered, about 20 minutes or until browned both sides and cooked as desired. Cover lamb; stand 10 minutes then slice thickly.

4 Meanwhile, make green bean salad. Make spiced yogurt.

5 Serve lamb with salad and yogurt.

GREEN BEAN SALAD Boil, steam or microwave beans until just tender; drain. Place in medium bowl with remaining ingredients; toss gently to combine.

SPICED YOGURT Combine ingredients in small bowl.

serves 4

per serving 21.5g carbohydrate; 18.8g total fat (3.3g saturated fat); 2216kJ (529 cal); 66.2g protein

carb tip Serve with a caramelised onion pilau.

grilled lamb steak with ratatouille

PREPARATION TIME 20 MINUTES **COOKING TIME** 25 MINUTES

1 Preheat oven to hot. Make balsamic dressing.

2 Combine vegetables and garlic, in single layer, in two large shallow baking dishes; coat vegetables lightly with cooking-oil spray. Cook, uncovered, in hot oven about 25 minutes or until ratatouille is just tender, stirring occasionally.

3 Meanwhile, cook lamb on heated oiled grill plate (or grill or barbecue) until cooked as desired.

4 Place ratatouille and half of the dressing in large bowl; toss gently to combine. Divide ratatouille and lamb among serving plates; drizzle with remaining dressing.

BALSAMIC DRESSING Place ingredients in screw-top jar; shake well.

serves 4
per serving 11g carbohydrate; 13.3g total fat (4.6g saturated fat); 1310kJ (313 cal); 36.5g protein
carb tip Serve with a warm baguette.

5 baby eggplants (300g), peeled, chopped coarsely

2 medium red capsicums (400g), chopped coarsely

1 medium yellow capsicum (200g), chopped coarsely

4 medium egg tomatoes (540g), chopped coarsely

1 medium brown onion (150g), chopped coarsely

2 cloves garlic, sliced thickly

cooking-oil spray

4 x 150g lamb steaks

BALSAMIC DRESSING

1 tablespoon olive oil

1 tablespoon lemon juice

1 tablespoon balsamic vinegar

1 clove garlic, crushed

¼ cup loosely packed fresh oregano leaves

teriyaki lamb stir-fry

PREPARATION TIME 15 MINUTES **COOKING TIME** 15 MINUTES

2 teaspoons olive oil

800g lean lamb strips

2 teaspoons sesame oil

2 cloves garlic, crushed

1 medium brown onion (150g),
   sliced thickly

1 fresh long red chilli,
   sliced thinly

⅓ cup (80ml) teriyaki sauce

¼ cup (60ml) sweet chilli sauce

500g baby bok choy, quartered

175g broccolini, chopped
   coarsely

1 Heat olive oil in wok; stir-fry lamb, in batches, until cooked as desired.

2 Heat sesame oil in same wok; stir-fry garlic, onion and chilli until fragrant. Add sauces; bring to a boil. Add bok choy and broccolini; stir-fry until bok choy just wilts and broccolini is just tender. Return lamb to wok; stir-fry until heated through.

serves 4

per serving 7.3g carbohydrate; 12.6g total fat (3.9g saturated fat); 1426kJ (341 cal); 48.4g protein

carb tip Serve with steamed long-grain rice.

pork

Tap the stem end of a cored iceberg lettuce soundly against the edge of your kitchen sink then hold the lettuce under cold running water; the leaves will fall off, one by one, intact.

sang choy bow

PREPARATION TIME 15 MINUTES **COOKING TIME** 10 MINUTES

1 tablespoon sesame oil
1 medium brown onion (150g), chopped finely
2 cloves garlic, crushed
300g pork mince
300g veal mince
¼ cup (60ml) soy sauce
¼ cup (60ml) oyster sauce
1 medium red capsicum (150g), chopped finely
3 cups (240g) bean sprouts
3 green onions, chopped coarsely
1 tablespoon toasted sesame seeds
8 large iceberg lettuce leaves

1 Heat oil in wok; stir-fry brown onion and garlic until onion softens. Add both minces; stir-fry until cooked through. Add sauces and capsicum, reduce heat; simmer, uncovered, stirring occasionally, 3 minutes.

2 Just before serving, stir in sprouts, green onion and seeds. Divide lettuce leaves among serving plates; spoon sang choy bow into leaves.

serves 4
per serving 10.1g carbohydrate; 17.2g total fat (4.9g saturated fat); 1463kJ (350 cal); 37.9g protein
carb tip Serve with fried chow mein noodles.

Baby vegetables, besides being visually appealing, are, as a rule, more tender, more subtly flavoured, quicker to cook and easier to prepare than their fully-grown counterparts.

pork steaks with beetroot salad

PREPARATION TIME 20 MINUTES **COOKING TIME** 45 MINUTES

300g baby beetroot
1 tablespoon caraway seeds
2 teaspoons olive oil
4 x 175g butterflied pork steaks
150g firm goat cheese, crumbled
5 large red radishes (175g), trimmed, sliced thinly
125g baby rocket leaves

DIJON VINAIGRETTE
2 teaspoons dijon mustard
2 teaspoons olive oil
2 tablespoons red wine vinegar

1 Preheat oven to moderately hot.
2 Discard beetroot stems and leaves; place unpeeled beetroot in small shallow baking dish. Roast, uncovered, in moderately hot oven about 45 minutes or until beetroot is tender. Cool 10 minutes; peel, cut into quarters.
3 Meanwhile, make dijon vinaigrette.
4 Using mortar and pestle, crush seeds and oil into smooth paste; rub into pork. Cook pork on heated lightly oiled grill plate (or grill or barbecue) until cooked as desired.
5 Place beetroot and vinaigrette in large bowl with cheese, radish and rocket; toss gently to combine. Serve pork with salad.

DIJON VINAIGRETTE Place ingredients in screw-top jar; shake well.

serves 4
per serving 7.4g carbohydrate; 23.5g total fat (8.7g saturated fat); 1804kJ (431 cal); 47.4g protein
carb tip Serve with thick crisp parsnip, kumara and potato chips.

Choy sum, one of the best known Asian greens, is often confused with another, gai larn or chinese broccoli. The best way to distinguish the two is to note that choy sum's flower is yellow while gai larn's is white.

pork, lime and peanut salad

PREPARATION TIME 25 MINUTES (PLUS REFRIGERATION TIME) **COOKING TIME** 15 MINUTES

¼ cup (60ml) lime juice
4cm piece fresh ginger (20g), grated
800g pork fillets, sliced thinly
500g choy sum, chopped coarsely
2 tablespoons water
2 medium carrots (240g), cut into matchsticks
½ cup firmly packed fresh basil leaves
1 cup firmly packed fresh coriander leaves
4 green onions, sliced thinly
¼ cup (35g) coarsely chopped toasted unsalted peanuts

SWEET CHILLI DRESSING
1 tablespoon fish sauce
1 tablespoon sweet chilli sauce
2 tablespoons lime juice
1 fresh small red thai chilli, chopped finely

1 Combine juice and ginger in large bowl, add pork; toss pork to coat in marinade. Cover; refrigerate 3 hours or overnight.
2 Make sweet chilli dressing.
3 Stir-fry pork, in batches, in heated lightly oiled wok until cooked as desired. Cover to keep warm. Stir-fry choy sum with the water in same wok until just wilted.
4 Place pork, choy sum and dressing in large bowl with carrot, herbs and onion; toss gently to combine. Sprinkle with nuts.

SWEET CHILLI DRESSING Place ingredients in screw-top jar; shake well.

serves 4
per serving 6.8g carbohydrate; 10.4g total fat (2.2g saturated fat);
1344kJ (321 cal); 48.8g protein
carb tip Serve with rice vermicelli.

vegetarian

The large, flat cultivated mushrooms used here have a rich, earthy flavour and are ideal for filling and barbecuing. They are often misnamed field mushrooms, a variety that grows wild on forest floors and is seldom available commercially.

grilled vegetable and ricotta stack

PREPARATION TIME 20 MINUTES **COOKING TIME** 30 MINUTES

2 baby eggplants (120g), sliced thickly lengthways
1 medium green capsicum (200g), sliced thickly lengthways
1 medium red capsicum (200g), sliced thickly lengthways
2 large zucchini (300g), sliced thickly lengthways
4 x 175g flat mushrooms, stems removed
2 cups (400g) ricotta cheese
2 cloves garlic, crushed
½ cup coarsely chopped fresh basil
2 tablespoons finely chopped fresh chives
1 tablespoon coarsely chopped fresh oregano
1 tablespoon finely grated lemon rind
2 tablespoons toasted pine nuts

SEMI-DRIED TOMATO PESTO
¼ cup (35g) drained semi-dried tomatoes, halved
½ cup firmly packed fresh basil leaves
2 tablespoons balsamic vinegar
2 tablespoons water

1 Cook eggplant, capsicums, zucchini and mushrooms, in batches, on heated oiled grill plate (or grill or barbecue) until tender.
2 Meanwhile, combine cheese, garlic, herbs and rind in medium bowl.
3 Make semi-dried tomato pesto.
4 Divide mushrooms, stem-side up, among serving plates; layer with cheese mixture then random slices of eggplant, zucchini and capsicums. Drizzle with pesto; sprinkle with nuts.

SEMI-DRIED TOMATO PESTO Blend or process tomato and basil until mixture forms a paste. With motor operating, gradually add combined vinegar and water in thin, steady stream until pesto is smooth.

serves 4
per serving 10.9g carbohydrate; 17.6g total fat (7.5g saturated fat);
1204kJ (288 cal); 21g protein
carb tip Serve with warm pumpkin bread.

vegetable curry with yogurt

PREPARATION TIME 25 MINUTES **COOKING TIME** 15 MINUTES

Patty-pan squash, sometimes called button squash or scallopini, have a pleasant nutty taste and are ideal for hollowing, filling and baking, or being cooked quickly over high heat in a stir-fry or on a grill plate with other vegetables.

2 teaspoons vegetable oil
4cm piece fresh ginger (20g), grated
3 green onions, sliced thinly
2 cloves garlic, crushed
1 long green chilli, chopped finely
¼ teaspoon ground cardamom
1 teaspoon garam masala
1 tablespoon curry powder
1 teaspoon ground turmeric
2 medium green apples (300g), grated coarsely
1 tablespoon lemon juice
2 cups (500ml) vegetable stock
½ small cauliflower (500g), cut into florets
4 yellow patty-pan squash (100g), halved
2 small green zucchini (180g), sliced thickly
150g baby spinach leaves
200g low-fat yogurt

1 Heat oil in large saucepan; cook ginger, onion, garlic, chilli, cardamom, garam masala, curry powder and turmeric until fragrant. Add apple, juice and stock; cook, uncovered, 5 minutes, stirring occasionally.
2 Add cauliflower, squash and zucchini; cook, uncovered, until vegetables are just tender. Remove from heat; stir spinach and yogurt into curry just before serving.

serves 4
per serving 14.5g carbohydrate; 3.6g total fat (0.7g saturated fat);
534kJ (128 cal); 8.5g protein
carb tip Serve with steamed basmati rice.

roasted vegetables with eggplant

PREPARATION TIME 20 MINUTES **COOKING TIME** 50 MINUTES

1 Preheat oven to hot.

2 Quarter capsicums; discard seeds and membranes. Using fork prick eggplants all over; divide among two lightly oiled baking dishes with garlic and capsicum, skin-side up. Roast vegetables, uncovered, in hot oven about 30 minutes or until skins blister. Cover capsicum pieces with plastic or paper for 5 minutes; peel away skin, slice thickly. Cover to keep warm.

3 When cool enough to handle, peel eggplants and garlic. Coarsely chop eggplants; finely chop garlic. Combine eggplant and garlic in medium bowl with juice and tahini; cover to keep warm.

4 Meanwhile, cook mushroom in large lightly oiled frying pan, stirring, until tender. Add tomatoes and squash; cook, covered, until tomatoes just soften.

5 Place okra onto oiled oven tray; spray with oil. Roast, uncovered, in hot oven about 20 minutes or until just tender.

6 Combine capsicum, tomato mixture and okra in large bowl with basil; divide among serving plates, top with eggplant mixture. Sprinkle with sumac; serve immediately.

1 large green capsicum (350g)
2 large red capsicums (700g)
2 large yellow capsicums (700g)
2 medium eggplants (600g)
2 cloves garlic, unpeeled
¼ cup (60ml) lemon juice
2 teaspoons tahini
350g mushrooms, sliced thickly
250g cherry tomatoes
12 yellow patty-pan
    squash (360g), halved
400g okra, trimmed
cooking-oil spray
¾ cup loosely packed fresh
    basil leaves
1 teaspoon sumac

serves 4
per serving 21.8g carbohydrate; 3.1g total fat (0.2g saturated fat);
759kJ (181 cal); 15.8g protein
carb tip Serve with chickpeas cooked with garlic and lemon juice.

mixed mushrooms with garlic and chives

PREPARATION TIME 15 MINUTES **COOKING TIME** 40 MINUTES

800g flat mushrooms
100g shiitake mushrooms
100g swiss brown mushrooms
150g oyster mushrooms
cooking-oil spray
¼ cup (60ml) red wine vinegar
1 tablespoon olive oil
2 cloves garlic, crushed
⅔ cup coarsely chopped
   fresh chives
2 cups loosely packed fresh
   flat-leaf parsley leaves
1 medium red onion (170g),
   sliced thinly

1 Preheat oven to slow.
2 Cut flat mushrooms coarsely into large pieces; combine with remaining mushrooms. Spread mushrooms, in single layer, in two large shallow baking dishes; spray mushrooms with oil. Cook, uncovered, in slow oven about 40 minutes or until tender.
3 Heat vinegar, oil and garlic in small saucepan, stirring, 1 minute. Place vinegar mixture in large bowl with mushrooms, chives, parsley and onion; toss gently to combine. Serve warm or cold.

serves 4
per serving 6.7g carbohydrate; 6.3g total fat (1g saturated fat); 552kJ (132 cal); 11.6g protein
carb tip Serve with crusty round of sourdough.

mixed vegetable and herb frittata

PREPARATION TIME 25 MINUTES **COOKING TIME** 20 MINUTES

1 Make tomato salad.
2 Heat oil in large frying pan; cook garlic and zucchini, stirring, until zucchini is just tender. Add mushroom and spinach; cook, stirring, until spinach is just wilted.
3 Beat eggs and egg whites in medium bowl; stir in basil.
4 Preheat grill.
5 Pour egg mixture into pan with vegetables; cook, uncovered, over medium heat about 10 minutes or until set. Sprinkle with cheese; place under preheated grill until frittata is browned lightly. Serve with salad.

TOMATO SALAD Combine tomatoes and basil in medium serving bowl. Stir in vinegar just before serving.

serves 4
per serving 4.6g carbohydrate; 8.5g total fat (2.6g saturated fat); 696kJ (166 cal); 17.2g protein
carb tip Serve with toasted italian bread.

2 teaspoons olive oil
2 cloves garlic, crushed
2 medium zucchini (240g), sliced thinly
100g swiss brown mushrooms, sliced thinly
180g baby spinach leaves
3 eggs
8 egg whites
¼ cup coarsely chopped fresh basil
¼ cup (20g) coarsely grated parmesan cheese

TOMATO SALAD
250g yellow teardrop tomatoes, halved
250g cherry tomatoes, halved
¼ cup loosely packed fresh baby basil leaves
2 tablespoons balsamic vinegar

pan-fried tofu with cabbage salad

PREPARATION TIME 20 MINUTES **COOKING TIME** 15 MINUTES

You need half a chinese cabbage for this recipe.

3 x 300g pieces fresh firm silken tofu

1 tablespoon finely chopped fresh lemon grass

2 fresh small red thai chillies, sliced thinly

1 medium red onion (170g), sliced thinly

1 cup (80g) bean sprouts

4 cups (320g) finely shredded chinese cabbage

¾ cup firmly packed fresh coriander leaves

SWEET AND SOUR DRESSING

⅓ cup (80ml) lime juice

2 teaspoons grated palm sugar

2 tablespoons soy sauce

1 Pat tofu all over with absorbent paper. Slice each tofu piece vertically into four slices. Place tofu slices, in single layer, on absorbent-paper-lined tray; cover tofu with more absorbent paper, stand at least 10 minutes.

2 Meanwhile, make sweet and sour dressing.

3 Cook tofu, in batches, in large heated lightly oiled frying pan until browned both sides.

4 Meanwhile, place remaining ingredients in large bowl; toss gently to combine.

5 Divide salad among serving plates; top with tofu, drizzle with dressing.

SWEET AND SOUR DRESSING Place ingredients in small jug; whisk until sugar dissolves.

serves 4
per serving 8.2g carbohydrate; 15.6g total fat (2.3g saturated fat); 1237kJ (295 cal); 29.9g protein
carb tip Toss crunchy fried noodles through cabbage salad.

We used a crumbly, fairly firm-textured blue cheese having a distinctively pungent bite to give a lift to the creaminess of the dressing; however, if you prefer a milder cheese, use one of the brie-like blues readily available at your local deli.

You need to soak twelve 25cm bamboo skewers in water for at least an hour before using to prevent them from splintering or scorching.

vegetable and tofu skewers

PREPARATION TIME 20 MINUTES **COOKING TIME** 15 MINUTES

200g swiss brown mushrooms
1 medium green capsicum (200g), chopped coarsely
1 medium red capsicum (200g), chopped coarsely
1 medium yellow capsicum (200g), chopped coarsely
3 baby eggplants (180g), chopped coarsely
350g piece firm tofu, diced into 3cm pieces
8 yellow patty-pan squash (200g), halved
100g baby rocket leaves

BLUE CHEESE DRESSING
50g blue cheese
2 tablespoons buttermilk
200g low-fat yogurt
1 small white onion (80g), grated finely
1 clove garlic, crushed
1 tablespoon finely chopped fresh chives
1 tablespoon lemon juice

1 Thread mushrooms, capsicums, eggplant, tofu and squash, alternately, onto skewers.
2 Cook skewers on heated lightly oiled grill plate (or grill or barbecue) until tofu is browned all over and vegetables are just tender.
3 Meanwhile, make blue cheese dressing.
4 Serve skewers on rocket; drizzle with dressing.

BLUE CHEESE DRESSING Crumble cheese into small bowl; stir in remaining ingredients.

serves 4
per serving 13.4g carbohydrate; 11.1g total fat (4.7g saturated fat);
1031kJ (246 cal); 22.8g protein
carb tip Serve with steamed couscous.

japanese omelette salad

PREPARATION TIME 20 MINUTES **COOKING TIME** 5 MINUTES

1 Make wasabi dressing.

2 Using vegetable peeler, slice daikon and carrots into thin strips. Place in large bowl with radish, cabbage, sprouts, ginger and three-quarters of the onion.

3 Combine egg, sauce and seaweed in small jug. Pour half of the egg mixture in large heated lightly oiled frying pan; cook, uncovered, until just set. Slide omelette onto plate; roll into cigar shape. Slice omelette roll into thin rings. Repeat with remaining egg mixture.

4 Add dressing to salad; toss gently to combine. Divide salad among serving bowls; top with omelette rings and remaining onion.

WASABI DRESSING Place ingredients in screw-top jar; shake well.

serves 4
per serving 10.4g carbohydrate; 6.2g total fat (1.7g saturated fat); 610kJ (146 cal); 11.7g protein
carb tip Serve with cold soba noodles.

1 medium daikon (600g)
2 medium carrots (240g)
6 large red radishes (210g), sliced thinly
1½ cups (120g) finely shredded red cabbage
1½ cups (120g) bean sprouts
2 tablespoons pink pickled ginger, sliced thinly
6 green onions, sliced thinly
4 eggs, beaten lightly
1 tablespoon soy sauce
½ sheet toasted seaweed (yaki-nori), sliced thinly

WASABI DRESSING
1 tablespoon pink pickled ginger juice
2 tablespoons soy sauce
1 tablespoon mirin
1 teaspoon wasabi paste

haloumi and grilled vegetable salad

PREPARATION TIME 25 MINUTES **COOKING TIME** 30 MINUTES

2 medium red capsicums (400g)

2 medium yellow capsicums (400g)

1 medium eggplant (300g),
  sliced thickly

cooking-oil spray

2 cloves garlic, crushed

350g haloumi cheese,
  sliced thinly

1 tablespoon lemon juice

1 small red onion (100g),
  sliced thinly

100g baby rocket leaves

¼ cup loosely packed fresh
  basil leaves

½ cup (80g) drained
  caperberries, rinsed

1 lemon, cut into wedges

LEMON DRESSING

⅓ cup (80ml) lemon juice

2 tablespoons olive oil

1 teaspoon sugar

1 Preheat grill.

2 Quarter capsicums; discard seeds and membranes. Roast under grill, skin-side up, until skin blisters and blackens. Cover capsicum pieces in plastic or paper for 5 minutes; peel away skin, slice thinly.

3 Place eggplant slices on oiled oven tray; spray with oil, sprinkle with half of the garlic. Cook under preheated grill, turning occasionally, about 15 minutes or until softened. Cool 10 minutes; slice into thick strips.

4 Meanwhile, make lemon dressing.

5 Combine cheese in small bowl with juice and remaining garlic. Cook cheese in heated lightly oiled large frying pan, turning occasionally, about 5 minutes or until browned both sides.

6 Meanwhile, place capsicum, eggplant and dressing in large bowl with onion, rocket, basil and caperberries; toss gently to combine.

7 Divide salad among serving plates; top with cheese and lemon wedges.

LEMON DRESSING Place ingredients in screw-top jar; shake well.

serves 4
per serving 14.5g carbohydrate; 26g total fat (11g saturated fat); 1630kJ (389 cal); 23.9g protein
carb tip Serve with polenta croûtons.

drinks

minted lemon grass and ginger iced tea

PREPARATION TIME 10 MINUTES
(PLUS REFRIGERATION TIME)

6 lemon grass and ginger tea bags
1 litre (4 cups) boiling water
2 tablespoons grated palm sugar
10cm stick (20g) fresh lemon grass, chopped finely
½ small orange (90g), sliced thinly
½ lemon, sliced thinly
¼ cup firmly packed fresh mint leaves, torn

1 Place tea bags and the boiling water in large heatproof jug; stand 5 minutes.
2 Discard tea bags. Add sugar, lemon grass, orange and lemon to jug; stir to combine. Refrigerate, covered, until cold.
3 Stir mint into cold tea; serve over ice.

makes 1 litre
per 250ml 8g carbohydrate; 0.1g total fat
(0g saturated fat); 147kJ (35 cal); 0.4g protein

tomato, carrot and red capsicum juice

PREPARATION TIME 10 MINUTES
(PLUS REFRIGERATION TIME)

1 medium red capsicum (250g), chopped coarsely
4 medium tomatoes (300g), chopped coarsely
2 medium carrots (240g), chopped coarsely
⅓ cup firmly packed fresh flat-leaf parsley leaves
1 cup (250ml) water
dash Tabasco

1 Blend or process ingredients, in batches, until pureed; strain through coarse sieve into large jug.
2 Stir in Tabasco; refrigerate, covered, until cold.

makes 1 litre
per 250ml 6.3g carbohydrate; 0.2g total fat
(0g saturated fat); 153kJ (37 cal); 2.1g protein

cucumber, celery, apple and spinach juice

PREPARATION TIME 10 MINUTES
(PLUS REFRIGERATION TIME)

1 telegraph cucumber (400g), chopped coarsely
2 trimmed celery stalks (200g), chopped coarsely
2 large green apples (400g), cored, chopped coarsely
50g baby spinach leaves, stems removed
1 cup (250ml) water
⅓ cup firmly packed fresh mint leaves

1 Blend or process ingredients, in batches, until pureed; strain through coarse sieve into large jug.
2 Refrigerate, covered, until cold.

makes 1 litre
per 250ml 11.1g carbohydrate; 0.3g total fat
(0g saturated fat); 228kJ (55 cal); 2g protein

citrus crush

PREPARATION TIME 10 MINUTES

2 medium limes, cut into wedges
2 medium lemons, cut into wedges
1 tablespoon brown sugar
½ cup firmly packed fresh mint leaves
4 cups crushed ice
500ml diet lemonade

1 Using mortar and pestle, crush lime, lemon, sugar and mint, in batches if necessary, until mixture is pulpy and sugar dissolved.
2 Combine citrus mixture in large jug with crushed ice. Stir lemonade into jug; serve immediately.

makes 1 litre
per 250ml 4.4g carbohydrate; 0.2g total fat
(0g saturated fat); 127kJ (30 cal); 0.6g protein

spiced iced coffee milkshake

PREPARATION TIME 10 MINUTES

¼ cup (20g) ground espresso coffee
¾ cup (180ml) boiling water
2 cardamom pods, bruised
¼ teaspoon ground cinnamon
1 tablespoon brown sugar
3 scoops (375ml) low-fat vanilla ice-cream
2½ cups (625ml) no-fat milk

1 Place coffee then the boiling water in coffee plunger; stand 2 minutes before plunging. Pour coffee into small heatproof bowl with cardamom, cinnamon and sugar; stir to dissolve sugar then cool 10 minutes.
2 Strain coffee mixture through fine sieve into blender or processor; process with ice-cream and milk until smooth. Serve immediately.

makes 1 litre
per 250ml 19.9g carbohydrate; 1.6g total fat
(1.1g saturated fat); 510kJ (122 cal); 7.9g protein

mixed berry smoothie

PREPARATION TIME 5 MINUTES

250ml frozen low-fat strawberry yogurt,
  softened slightly
1⅓ cups (200g) frozen mixed berries
3 cups (750ml) no-fat milk

1 Blend or process ingredients, in batches, until smooth. Serve immediately.

makes 1 litre
per 250ml 25.7g carbohydrate; 3.6g total fat
(2.3g saturated fat); 724kJ (173 cal); 10.2g protein

banana passionfruit soy smoothie

PREPARATION TIME 10 MINUTES
(PLUS REFRIGERATION TIME)

You need about six passionfruit for this recipe.

½ cup (125ml) passionfruit pulp
2 cups (500ml) no-fat soy milk
2 medium ripe bananas (400g), chopped coarsely

1 Strain pulp through sieve into small bowl; reserve liquid and seeds.
2 Blend or process passionfruit liquid, milk and banana, in batches, until smooth.
3 Pour smoothie into large jug; stir in reserved seeds. Refrigerate, covered, until cold.

makes 1 litre
per 250ml 19.9g carbohydrate; 0.6g total fat
(0g saturated fat); 443kJ (106 cal); 5.3g protein

pineapple orange frappé

PREPARATION TIME 10 MINUTES

1 medium pineapple (1.25kg), chopped coarsely
½ cup (125ml) orange juice
3 cups crushed ice
1 tablespoon finely grated orange rind

1 Blend or process pineapple and juice, in batches, until smooth.
2 Pour into large jug with crushed ice and rind; stir to combine. Serve immediately.

makes 1 litre
per 250ml 15.7g carbohydrate; 0.2g total fat
(0g saturated fat); 306kJ (73 cal); 1.8g protein

glossary

ARTICHOKES

globe large flower-bud of a member of the thistle family; having tough petal-like leaves, edible in part when cooked.

hearts tender centre of the globe artichoke. Artichoke hearts can be fresh from the plant or purchased in brine canned or in glass jars.

BEETROOT also known as red beets or just beets; firm, round root vegetable.

BOK CHOY also known as bak choy, pak choy, chinese white cabbage; has a mild mustard taste. Baby bok choy is smaller and more tender, and often cooked whole.

BROCCOLINI a cross between broccoli and chinese kale; is milder and sweeter than traditional broccoli. Substitute chinese broccoli (gai larn) or common broccoli.

BUTTERMILK sold alongside fresh milk products in supermarkets; despite the implication of its name, it is low in fat.

CABBAGE

chinese also known as peking cabbage, wong bok or petsai. It is elongated in shape with pale green, crinkly leaves.

savoy large, heavy head with crinkled dark-green outer leaves; a fairly mild-tasting cabbage.

CAPERBERRIES fruit formed after caper buds have flowered; sold pickled with stalks intact.

CAPERS the grey-green buds of a warm climate (usually Mediterranean) shrub; sold either dried and salted or pickled in a vinegar brine. **Baby capers** are smaller, fuller-flavoured and more expensive than the full-sized ones.

CAPSICUM also known as bell pepper or, simply, pepper. Discard seeds and membranes before use. Capsicums come in many colours, red, green, yellow, orange and purplish-black.

CARAWAY SEEDS a member of the parsley family; available in seed or ground form, and appropriate for sweet or savoury dishes.

CARDAMOM native to India and used extensively in its cuisine; can be purchased in pod, seed or ground form. Has a distinctive aromatic, sweetly rich flavour and is one of the world's most expensive spices.

CHEESE

bocconcini walnut-sized, fresh, baby mozzarella; a semi-soft, white cheese traditionally made in Italy from buffalo milk. Spoils rapidly, so must be kept under refrigeration, in brine, for 1 or 2 days at most.

cheddar the most widely eaten cheese in the world; a semi-hard cow-milk cheese originally made in England. We used a low-fat variety with not more than 7% fat content.

fetta a crumbly goat- or sheep-milk cheese with sharp salty taste.

goat made from goat milk, has an earthy, strong taste; available in both soft and firm textures, in various shapes and sizes, and sometimes rolled in ash or herbs.

haloumi a firm, cream-coloured sheep-milk cheese matured in brine; can be grilled or fried, briefly, without breaking down.

mozzarella a soft cheese having an elastic texture when heated; it is better suited for cooking than for eating on its own.

parmesan a hard, grainy cow-milk cheese mainly grated as a topping for pasta, soups and other savoury dishes, but is also delicious eaten with fruit. Also known as parmigiano.

ricotta a sweet, moist cheese with a fat content of around 8.5% and a slightly grainy texture

CHINESE BROCCOLI also known as gai larn or chinese kale; appreciated more for its stems than its coarse leaves. Can be served steamed and stir-fried, in soups and noodle dishes.

CHOY SUM also known as flowering bok choy or flowering white cabbage; easy to identify with its long stems, light green leaves and yellow flowers.

CORIANDER bright-green-leafed herb with a pungent flavour. Also known as cilantro or chinese parsley.

CORNICHONS French for gherkin; a very small variety of cucumber.

CURLY ENDIVE also known as frisee, a curly-leafed green vegetable, mainly used in salads.

DAIKON also called giant white radish. Sweet, fresh flavour with crisp, juicy and white flesh. The skin can be creamy white or black. Choose those that are firm and unwrinkled. Refrigerate, wrapped in a plastic bag, up to a week.

EGGPLANT purple-skinned vegetable also known as aubergine.

FIVE-SPICE POWDER a fragrant mixture of ground cinnamon, star anise, cloves, sichuan pepper and fennel seeds.

FLOUR

plain an all-purpose flour, made from wheat.

self-raising plain or wholemeal flour combined with baking powder in the proportion of 1 cup flour to 2 teaspoons baking powder.

GALANGAL also known as ka, a rhizome with a hot ginger-citrusy flavour. Sometimes known as thai, siamese or laos ginger, it also comes in a dried powdered form called laos. Fresh ginger can be substituted, but the flavour of the dish will not be the same.

GARAM MASALA literally meaning blended spices; a masala can be whole spices, a paste or a powder, and can include herbs as well as spices and other seasonings.

GINGER also known as green or root ginger; the thick gnarled root of a tropical plant. Can be kept, peeled, covered with dry sherry in a jar and refrigerated, or frozen in an airtight container.

GREEN PEPPERCORNS soft, unripe berry of the pepper plant; usually sold packed in brine.

HAM we used light ham with a fat content of approximately 4%, about half that of regular leg ham.

HARISSA sauce or paste made from dried red chillies, garlic, oil and sometimes caraway seeds.

KAFFIR LIME LEAVES also known as bai magrood; looks like two glossy dark-green leaves joined end to end, forming a rounded hourglass shape. Sold fresh, dried or frozen; the dried leaves are less potent so double the number called for in a recipe if you substitute them for fresh leaves. A strip of fresh lime peel may be substituted for each kaffir lime leaf.

KECAP MANIS Indonesian sweet, thick soy sauce that has sugar and spices added.

LEMON GRASS a tall, clumping, lemon-smelling and -tasting, sharp-edged grass; the white lower part of each stem is chopped and used in Asian cooking or for tea.

LYCHEES delicious fruit with a light texture and flavour; peel away rough skin, remove seed and use. Also available in cans.

MANGO tropical fruit originally from India or South-East Asia, with skin colour ranging from green through yellow to deep red. Fragrant deep yellow flesh surrounds a large flat seed. Mango cheeks in a light syrup are available canned.

MESCLUN a mixture of assorted young lettuce and other green leaves, including mizuna, baby spinach and curly endive.

MILK, LOW-FAT we used milk with 0.15% fat content or lower.

MIRIN a champagne-coloured Japanese cooking wine made of glutinous rice and alcohol. Used expressly for cooking and should not be confused with sake. There is a seasoned sweet mirin called manjo mirin that is made of water, rice, corn syrup and alcohol.

MUSHROOMS

button small, cultivated white mushrooms having a delicate, subtle flavour.

flat large, flat mushrooms with a rich earthy flavour, ideal for filling and barbecuing. Are sometimes misnamed field mushrooms, which are wild mushrooms.

portobello mature swiss browns. Large, dark-brown mushrooms with full-bodied flavour, ideal for filling or barbecuing.

shiitake when fresh are also known as chinese black, forest or golden oak mushrooms; although cultivated, have the earthiness and taste of wild mushrooms. Are large and meaty; often used as a substitute for meat in some Asian vegetarian dishes. When dried, they are known as donko or dried chinese mushrooms; rehydrate before use.

swiss brown also known as cremini or roman mushrooms. Light to dark-brown mushrooms with full-bodied flavour. Button or cup mushrooms can be substituted for swiss brown mushrooms.

MUSTARD

dijon a pale brown, distinctively flavoured fairly mild french mustard.

mild english less pungent version of traditional hot english mustard.

NUTS

almonds, blanched skins removed.

almonds, slivered small lengthways-cut pieces.

cashews we used unsalted roasted cashews.

pine nuts not, in fact, a nut, but a small, cream-coloured kernel from pine cones. Also known as pignoli.

OIL

cooking-oil spray we used a cholesterol-free cooking spray made from canola oil.

olive oil made from ripened olives. Extra virgin and virgin are the best, while extra light or light refers to taste not fat levels.

peanut pressed from ground peanuts; most commonly used oil in Asian cooking because of its high smoke point (capacity to handle high heat without burning).

sesame made from roasted, crushed, white sesame seeds.

OKRA
also known as bamia or lady fingers; a green, ridged, oblong pod with a furry skin. Native to Africa, this vegetable is used in Indian, Middle-Eastern and southern US cooking. Often serves as a thickener in stews.

ONIONS

brown and white these are interchangeable. Their pungent flesh adds flavour to a vast range of dishes.

green also known as scallion or, incorrectly, shallot; an immature onion picked before the bulb has formed, having a long, bright-green edible stalk.

red also known as spanish, red spanish or bermuda onion; a sweet-flavoured, large, purple-red onion that is particularly good eaten in raw salads.

PAPRIKA
ground dried red capsicum (bell pepper), available sweet or hot.

PARSLEY, FLAT-LEAF
also known as continental parsley or italian parsley.

PATTY-PAN SQUASH
also known as crookneck or custard marrow pumpkins; a round, slightly flat summer squash being yellow to pale-green in colour and having a scalloped edge. Harvested young, it has firm, white flesh and distinct flavour.

SALTED BLACK BEANS
also known as chinese black beans; these are fermented and salted soy beans available in cans and jars. Used most often in Asian cooking; chop before, or mash during cooking to release flavour.

SAUCES

fish also called nam pla or nuoc nam; made from pulverised salted fermented fish, most often anchovies. Has a pungent smell and strong taste; use sparingly.

hoisin a thick, sweet and spicy Chinese paste made from salted fermented soy beans, onions and garlic; used as a marinade or baste, or to accent stir-fries and barbecued or roasted foods.

oyster Asian in origin, this rich, brown sauce is made from oysters and their brine, cooked with salt and soy sauce then thickened.

soy made from fermented soy beans. Several variations are available in most supermarkets and Asian food stores.

sweet chilli a comparatively mild, Thai-style sauce made from red chillies, sugar, garlic and vinegar.

Tabasco brand name of an extremely fiery sauce made from vinegar, hot red peppers and salt.

SHALLOTS
also known as french shallots, golden shallots or eschalots; small, elongated, brown-skinned members of the onion family. Grows in tight clusters similar to garlic.

SILVERBEET
member of the beet family. A green-leafed vegetable with sturdy celery-like white stems; also known as swiss chard and, incorrectly, spinach. Can be used similarly to spinach.

SNOWPEAS
also known as snow pea sprouts or mange tout (eat all).

SOUR CREAM, LIGHT
we used a low-fat sour cream having 18.5% fat content.

SPINACH
also known as english spinach and, incorrectly, silverbeet. Tender green leaves are good uncooked in salads or added to soups, stir-fries and stews just before serving.

STAR ANISE
a dried star-shaped pod whose seeds have an astringent aniseed flavour; used to favour stocks and marinades.

SUGAR
we used coarse granulated table sugar, also known as crystal sugar, unless otherwise specified.

brown an extremely soft, fine granulated sugar retaining molasses for its characteristic colour and flavour.

caster also known as superfine or finely granulated table sugar.

palm also known as nam tan pip, jaggery, jawa or gula melaka; made from the sap of the sugar palm tree. Light brown to black in colour and usually sold in rock-hard cakes; may be substituted with brown sugar.

SUMAC
a purple-red, astringent spice ground from berries growing on shrubs that flourish wild around the Mediterranean; adds a lemony, tart flavour to dips and dressings and goes well with barbecued meat. Can be found in Middle-Eastern food stores. *Substitute*: ½ teaspoon lemon pepper + 1/8 teaspoon five spice + 1/8 teaspoon allspice equals ¾ teaspoon sumac.

TAHINI
sesame-seed paste available from Middle-Eastern food stores; most often used in hummus, baba ghanoush and other Lebanese recipes.

TAMARIND CONCENTRATE
made from the pods of a tree native to India that contain a sour-sweet pulp, which can be dried and reconstituted to make a dark, thick paste that adds an astringent, tangy taste to curries. It can also be used in marinades and bastes for meats.

TAT SOI
also known as rosette bok choy; a dark-leafed variety of bok choy. Developed to grow close to the ground so it is easily protected from frost.

TOFU
also known as bean curd; an off-white, custard-like product made from the milk of crushed soy beans; comes fresh as soft or firm, and processed as fried or pressed dried sheets. Leftover fresh tofu can be refrigerated in water (which is changed daily) for up to four days. **Silken tofu** refers to the manufacturing method of straining the soy bean liquid through silk

TOMATO

cherry also known as Tiny Tim or Tom Thumb; small and round.

egg also called Plum or Roma; smallish, oval-shaped tomatoes most often used in Italian cooking.

semi-dried partially dried tomato pieces in olive oil; softer and juicier than sun-dried tomatoes.

sun-dried we used sun-dried tomatoes packaged in oil, unless otherwise specified.

truss small vine-ripened tomatoes with vine still attached.

TURMERIC
also known as kamin; a rhizome related to galangal and ginger. Must be grated or pounded to release its somewhat acrid aroma and pungent flavour. Known for the golden colour it imparts to dishes. Fresh turmeric can be substituted with the more common dried powder (use 2 teaspoons of ground turmeric plus a teaspoon of sugar for every 20g of fresh turmeric called for in a recipe).

VIETNAMESE MINT LEAVES
not a mint at all; this narrow-leafed, pungent herb, also known as cambodian mint and laksa leaf (daun laksa), is widely used in many Asian soups and salads.

VINEGAR

balsamic authentic only from the province of Modena, Italy; made from a regional wine of white Trebbiano grapes specially processed then aged in antique wooden casks to give the exquisite pungent flavour.

rice a colourless vinegar made from fermented rice and flavoured with sugar and salt. Also known as seasoned rice vinegar. Sherry can be substituted.

red wine based on fermented red wine.

white wine made from white wine.

WASABI
an Asian horseradish used to make the pungent, green-coloured sauce traditionally served with Japanese raw fish dishes; sold in powdered or paste form.

WITLOF
also known as chicory or belgian endive.

YAKI-NORI (NORI)
a type of dried seaweed used in Japanese cooking. Sold in thin sheets.

YOGURT, LOW-FAT
we used yogurt having a fat content of less than 0.2%.

ZUCCHINI
also known as courgettes. Small green, yellow or white vegetable belonging to the squash family; has edible flowers.

index

facts + figures

Wherever you live, you'll be able to use our recipes with the help of these easy-to-follow conversions. While these conversions are approximate only, the difference between an exact and the approximate conversion of various liquid and dry measures is minimal and will not affect your cooking results.

liquid measures

metric	imperial
30ml	1 fluid oz
60ml	2 fluid oz
100ml	3 fluid oz
125ml	4 fluid oz
150ml	5 fluid oz (¼ pint/1 gill)
190ml	6 fluid oz
250ml	8 fluid oz
300ml	10 fluid oz (½ pint)
500ml	16 fluid oz
600ml	20 fluid oz (1 pint)
1000ml (1 litre)	1¾ pints

measuring equipment

The difference between one country's measuring cups and another's is, at most, within a 2 or 3 teaspoon variance. (For the record, one Australian metric measuring cup holds approximately 250ml.) The most accurate way of measuring dry ingredients is to weigh them. When measuring liquids, use a clear glass or plastic jug with the metric markings. (One Australian metric tablespoon holds 20ml; one Australian metric teaspoon holds 5ml.)

dry measures

metric	imperial
15g	½oz
30g	1oz
60g	2oz
90g	3oz
125g	4oz (¼lb)
155g	5oz
185g	6oz
220g	7oz
250g	8oz (½lb)
280g	9oz
315g	10oz
345g	11oz
375g	12oz (¾lb)
410g	13oz
440g	14oz
470g	15oz
500g	16oz (1lb)
750g	24oz (1½lb)
1kg	32oz (2lb)

helpful measures

metric	imperial
3mm	⅛in
6mm	¼in
1cm	½in
2cm	¾in
2.5cm	1in
5cm	2in
6cm	2½in
8cm	3in
10cm	4in
13cm	5in
15cm	6in
18cm	7in
20cm	8in
23cm	9in
25cm	10in
28cm	11in
30cm	12in (1ft)

how to measure

When using graduated metric measuring cups, shake dry ingredients loosely into the appropriate cup. Do not tap the cup on a bench or tightly pack the ingredients unless directed to do so. Level top of measuring cups and measuring spoons with a knife. When measuring liquids, place a clear glass or plastic jug with metric markings on a flat surface to check accuracy at eye level.

Note: North America, NZ and the UK use 15ml tablespoons. All cup and spoon measurements are level.

We use large eggs having an average weight of 60g.

oven temperatures

These oven temperatures are only a guide. Always check the manufacturer's manual.

	°C (Celsius)	°F (Fahrenheit)	Gas Mark
Very slow	120	250	½
Slow	140 – 150	275 – 300	1 – 2
Moderately slow	170	325	3
Moderate	180 – 190	350 – 375	4 – 5
Moderately hot	200	400	6
Hot	220 – 230	425 – 450	7 – 8
Very hot	240	475	9

ARE YOU MISSING SOME OF THE WORLD'S FAVOURITE COOKBOOKS?

The Australian Women's Weekly Cookbooks are available from bookshops, cookshops, supermarkets and other stores all over the world. You can also buy direct from the publisher, using the order form below.

TITLE	RRP	QTY	TITLE	RRP	QTY
Almost Vegetarian	£5.99		French Food, New	£5.99	
Asian Meals in Minutes	£5.99		Get Real, Make a Meal	£5.99	
Babies & Toddlers Good Food	£5.99		Good Food Fast	£5.99	
Barbecue Meals In Minutes	£5.99		Great Beef Cookbook	£5.99	
Basic Cooking Class	£5.99		Great Chicken Cookbook	£5.99	
Beginners Cooking Class	£5.99		Great Lamb Cookbook	£5.99	
Beginners Simple Meals	£5.99		Greek Cooking Class	£5.99	
Beginners Thai	£5.99		Healthy Heart Cookbook	£5.99	
Best Ever Slimmers' Recipes	£5.99		Indian Cooking Class	£5.99	
Best Food	£5.99		Italian Cooking Class	£5.99	
Best Food Desserts	£5.99		Japanese Cooking Class	£5.99	
Best Food Mains	£5.99		Kids' Birthday Cakes	£5.99	
Big Book of Beautiful Biscuits	£5.99		Kids Cooking	£5.99	
Biscuits & Slices	£5.99		Lean Food	£5.99	
Cakes & Slices Cookbook	£5.99		Low-fat Feasts	£5.99	
Cakes Cooking Class	£5.99		Low-fat Food For Life	£5.99	
Caribbean Cooking	£5.99		Low-fat Meals in Minutes	£5.99	
Casseroles	£5.99		Main Course Salads	£5.99	
Celebration Cakes	£5.99		Meals in Minutes	£5.99	
Chicken Meals in Minutes	£5.99		Mediterranean Cookbook	£5.99	
Chinese Cooking Class	£5.99		Middle Eastern Cooking Class	£5.99	
Christmas Book	£5.99		Midweek Meals in Minutes	£5.99	
Christmas Cooking	£5.99		Muffins, Scones & Bread	£5.99	
Cocktails	£5.99		New Finger Food	£5.99	
Cooking for Crowds	£5.99		Pasta Cookbook	£5.99	
Cooking for Friends	£5.99		Pasta Meals in Minutes	£5.99	
Cooking For Two	£5.99		Potatoes	£5.99	
Creative Cooking on a Budget	£5.99		Quick Meals in Minutes	£5.99	
Detox (Sept 05)	£5.99		Quick-mix Biscuits & Slices	£5.99	
Dinner Beef	£5.99		Quick-mix Cakes	£5.99	
Dinner Lamb (Aug 05)	£5.99		Salads: Simple, Fast & Fresh	£5.99	
Dinner Seafood	£5.99		Saucery	£5.99	
Easy Australian Style	£5.99		Sensational Stir-Fries	£5.99	
Easy Curry	£5.99		Short-order Cook	£5.99	
Easy Spanish-Style	£5.99		Sweet Old Fashioned Favourites	£5.99	
Easy Vietnamese-Style	£5.99		Thai Cooking Class	£5.99	
Essential Barbecue	£5.99		Vegetarian Meals in Minutes	£5.99	
Essential Microwave	£5.99		Weekend Cook	£5.99	
Essential Soup	£5.99		Wicked Sweet Indulgences	£5.99	
Freezer, Meals from the	£5.99		Wok Meals in Minutes	£5.99	
French Cooking Class	£5.99		**TOTAL COST:**	**£**	

NAME

ADDRESS

POSTCODE

DAYTIME PHONE

I ENCLOSE MY CHEQUE/MONEY ORDER FOR £

OR PLEASE CHARGE MY VISA, ACCESS OR MASTERCARD NUMBER

CARD HOLDER'S NAME

EXPIRY DATE

CARDHOLDER'S SIGNATURE

To order: Mail or fax — photocopy or complete the order form above, and send your credit card details or cheque payable to: Australian Consolidated Press (UK), Moulton Park Business Centre, Red House Road, Moulton Park, Northampton NN3 6AQ, phone (+44) (0) 1604 497531, fax (+44) (0) 1604 497533, e-mail books@acpuk.com
Non-UK residents: We accept the credit cards listed on the coupon, or cheques, drafts or International Money Orders payable in sterling and drawn on a UK bank. Credit card charges are at the exchange rate current at the time of payment.
Postage and packing: Within the UK, add £1.50 for one book or £3.00 for two books. There is no postal charge for orders of three or more books for delivery within the UK. For delivery outside the UK, please phone, fax or e-mail for a quote.
Offer ends 31.12.2005

Test Kitchen
Food director *Pamela Clark*
Food editor *Karen Hammial*
Assistant food editor *Amira Georgy*
Test Kitchen manager *Cathie Lonnie*
Home economists *Sammie Coryton,*
Nancy Duran, Benjamin Haslam,
Elizabeth Macri, Christina Martignago,
Sharon Reeve, Susie Riggall, Kirrily Smith
Editorial coordinator *Rebecca Steyns*
Nutritional information *Laila Ibram*

ACP Books
Editorial director *Susan Tomnay*
Creative director *Hieu Chi Nguyen*
Senior editor *Wendy Bryant*
Designer *Hieu Chi Nguyen*
Studio manager *Caryl Wiggins*
Design assistant *Josii Do*
Editorial coordinator *Merryn Pearse*
Sales director *Brian Cearnes*
Publishing manager (rights & new projects)
 Jane Hazell
Marketing director *Nicole Pizanis*
Marketing manager *Katie Graham*
Brand manager *Renée Crea*
Sales and marketing coordinator *Gabrielle Botto*
Pre-press *Harry Palmer*
Production manager *Carol Currie*
Business manager *Seymour Cohen*
Assistant business analyst *Martin Howes*
Chief executive officer *John Alexander*
Group publisher *Pat Ingram*
Publisher *Sue Wannan*
Editor-in-chief *Deborah Thomas*

Produced by ACP Books, Sydney.
Printed by Dai Nippon Printing in Korea.
Published by ACP Publishing Pty Limited, 54 Park St, Sydney; GPO Box 4088, Sydney, NSW 2001.
Ph: (02) 9282 8618 Fax: (02) 9267 9438.
www.acpbooks.com.au
To order books, phone 136 116.
Send recipe enquiries to:
recipeenquiries@acp.com.au
AUSTRALIA: Distributed by Network Services, GPO Box 4088, Sydney, NSW 2001.
Ph: (02) 9282 8777 Fax: (02) 9264 3278.
UNITED KINGDOM: Distributed by Australian Consolidated Press (UK), Moulton Park Business Centre, Red House Rd, Moulton Park, Northampton, NN3 6AQ.
Ph: (01604) 497 531 Fax: (01604) 497 533 acpukltd@aol.com
CANADA: Distributed by Whitecap Books Ltd, 351 Lynn Ave, North Vancouver, BC, V7J 2C4.
Ph: (604) 980 9852 Fax: (604) 980 8197 customerservice@whitecap.ca
www.whitecap.ca
NEW ZEALAND: Distributed by Netlink Distribution Company, ACP Media Centre, Cnr Fanshawe and Beaumont Streets, Westhaven, Auckland.
PO Box 47906, Ponsonby, Auckland, NZ.
Ph: (09) 366 9966 ask@ndcnz.co.nz
SOUTH AFRICA: Distributed by PSD Promotions, 30 Diesel Road, Isando, Gauteng, Johannesburg. PO Box 1175, Isando 1600, Gauteng, Johannesburg.
Ph: (2711) 392 6065/6/7
Fax: (2711) 392 6079/80
orders@psdprom.co.za

Clark, Pamela.
Low-carb, low-fat.

Includes index.
ISBN 1 86396 383 9.

1. Cookery. 2. Low-carbohydrate diet – Recipes.
I. Australian Women's Weekly. II. Title.

641.5638

© ACP Publishing Pty Limited 2004
ABN 18 053 273 546

The publishers would like to thank the following for props used in photography:
Atmosphere, Surry Hills; Living Edge, Surry Hills; Stem, Balmain; Wheel and Barrow.